Forgiving Yourself
By Julie Anshasi

Giant Publishing Company
Lincoln, Nebraska, USA

2021 by Julie Anshasi

Published by Giant Publishing Company
Post Office Box 6455
Lincoln, NE 68506
www.giantpublishingcompany.com

Printed in the United States of America

All scripture quotations are from the King James Version of the Bible, unless otherwise noted.

Library of Congress Cataloging-in-Publication Data
Anshasi, Julie, 1963 -
Forgiving Yourself   self-help/Julie Anshasi
    1. Christianity
    2. Self-help
TX0009015986

ISBN 978-1-7352827-3-2

Cover photo courtesy of Eric Torres.

To Julie:

Please do not feel completely, totally, irrevocably,
solely, irreversibly, and unilaterally responsible for
everything.
That's My job.
Love,
God

Books by Julie Anshasi

Broken ~ Poems from the Holy Spirit
Copyright 2017 – Winner of the 2021 Illumination Book Awards Silver Medal

Some Things are HOT! Some Things are NOT!
Copyright 2018

Behind the Word: Bible Stories to Ignite Your Imagination
Copyright 2018

Why Did the Dinosaurs Die?
Copyright 2019

Winter in Eden
Copyright 2020 – Winner of the 2022 Illumination Book Awards Bronze Medal

The Revelation of Jesus Christ
Copyright 2020

One Part Nonsense
Copyright 2020

Spiritual Exhaustion
Copyright 2021 - Winner of the 2022 Illumination Book Awards Silver Medal

Lame for Life
Copyright 2022

Quiet ~ A devotional
Copyright 2022

Table of Contents

Introduction

We have all heard that a lack of forgiveness will destroy us. We all know, intellectually at least, that we must forgive. The Lord's prayer tells us that God will forgive us in the same manner in which we forgive others. So, we try to forgive those who have wronged us.

Unfortunately, many of us cannot forgive ourselves.

If you are carrying the burden of unforgiveness toward yourself, you are living a life of imprisonment. You need help and healing. You need to be set free.

This book chronicles the stories of Bible characters from long ago, and people that I have personally come in contact with, who have struggled with self-forgiveness. Modern-day names have been changed in this book, in order to protect the people's privacy. Some of these people were ultimately able to forgive themselves. Most were not.

It is my hope that the glorious light of God will break through the darkness that has been surrounding you, that you will know His great compassion toward you, and that you will be able to reach out and embrace His forgiveness, which in turn will enable you to forgive yourself.

– Julie Anshasi
Author, Bible teacher, winner of multiple Illumination
Book Awards - 2021

The people that walked in darkness have seen a great light: they that dwell in the land of the shadow of death, upon them hath the light shined. Isaiah 9:2

Chapter 1: Murder and suicide

Is one sin worse than another?

For all have sinned, and come short of the glory of God.
Romans 3:23

As Christians, we know that God does not put sins into categories of "greater" or "lesser." If He did, it would mean that some people are in greater need of a Savior than others. But God doesn't see it that way.

As   it is written, There is none righteous,   no,   not   one: There   is   none   that   understandeth,   there   is   none   that seeketh after God. They are all gone out of the way, they are   together   become   unprofitable;   there   is   none   that doeth good, no, not one.   Romans 3:10-12

But when we examine our own hearts, and attempt to examine the hearts of those around us, we often end up comparing ourselves to others, in an attempt to justify our own actions. Something I have heard over and over is, "Well, at least I haven't killed anyone."

But what if you *have* killed someone?

And Cain talked with Abel his brother: and it came to pass, when they were in the field, that Cain rose up against   Abel   his   brother,   and   slew   him.   And the LORD said unto Cain, Where is Abel thy brother? And he said, I know not: Am I my brother's keeper? Genesis 4:8 - 9

Cain killed his own brother, Abel, because he was jealous of him. He then pretended not to know anything about it.

And (God) said, What hast thou done? the voice of thy brother's blood crieth unto me from the ground. And now art thou cursed from the earth, which hath opened her mouth to receive thy brother's blood from thy hand; When thou tillest the ground, it shall not henceforth yield unto thee her strength; a fugitive and a vagabond shalt thou be in the earth. And Cain said unto the LORD, My punishment is greater than I can bear. Genesis 4:10 - 13

I want to focus on Cain's words here. "My punishment is greater than I can bear."

Cain was unable to bear the thought of being cut off from his family and his people. Until then, he had known only the comfort of his immediate family. We can infer that his family was quite large, but we can also infer that they were a tight-knit group. Now, God was saying that because Cain had committed murder, he was to be cut off from them, to live life as a fugitive. It was more than he could bear.

***

Janie is someone who comes to mind when I think about Cain. After having an abortion, she was not able to live a normal life in society with "normal" people. Janie suffered from what a psychiatrist would call post-traumatic stress disorder.

"I thought that there was no way that God could forgive me for having an abortion," Janie said. "I thought it was the worst thing a person could do. I started feeling afraid all the time, looking over my shoulder, thinking God was going to strike me dead at any time. I thought I had to live a perfect life to show Him that I was a good person."

Janie had been raised in a Christian home, and she knew that salvation was by grace alone, not by any good deeds that she could do. Still, the abortion haunted her. She kept saying to herself, over and over, "What can be worse than murder?"

Janie's experience is very common. Women who have had abortions suffer nightmares, panic attacks, and severe depression. Another common side effect of abortion is hallucinations. A post-abortive woman will often hear a baby crying, when there is no baby around. She will re-live the physical pain of the abortion in her body, again and again, although she is not actually in pain in those moments.

Women who have had an abortion commit suicide at a staggeringly higher rate than those who have never had an abortion. One U.S. study put the risk of suicide after abortion at 154% higher than that of the general population.

It is telling that even with these widespread statistics, Planned Parenthood still refuses to offer counseling to post-abortive women.

Janie received a miraculous touch of the Holy Spirit which enabled her to forgive herself for having an abortion. She now knows that God is able to forgive any sin, if we turn to Him with a repentant heart.

Men who have lost their children through abortion suffer also. Some men don't find out that an abortion has occurred until after the fact, when it is too late to do anything to stop it. Others pressure or coerce their partners into having an abortion. While post-abortive women typically experience extreme grief over what they have done, post-abortive men often react with anger.

"I blamed her," said Andy, whose girlfriend had an unplanned pregnancy. "She was careless. She should have known better and taken better precautions."

Andy gave his girlfriend a choice. It was either him or the baby. Because she loved him so much and didn't want to lose him, she aborted their child.

After the abortion, their relationship was marked by Andy's outbursts of anger and impatience. He couldn't understand why she couldn't just "get over it," and every time he saw her crying, he yelled at her. What he didn't realize at the time was that he was carrying a huge load of guilt and shame over forcing her to have the abortion. Her tears were a constant reminder to him of what he had done. Because he was unable to forgive himself, he took it out on her.

Like many couples who go through abortion, their relationship didn't last.

Glen's father committed suicide when he was a young boy. It was during the depression, and in those days, suicide was rarely, if ever, talked about. Glen not only had to live without his father, he had to live with the secret of how his father died. As the oldest child, he blamed himself for his father's death, even though it had nothing to do with him and there was nothing he could have done to prevent it. He spent his life wondering, "What if?"

Satan is a very crafty person. First, he tempts you to sin, then, when you give in to the temptation, he tells you how rotten you are for sinning. Finally, when you feel so terrible for being such a rotten person, he convinces you that suicide is the only possible escape from yourself and your rottenness.

Glen never came to terms with his father's suicide. Self-murder has been described as the most selfish act a person can commit, because it leaves in its wake a trail of shattered family members and friends searching for answers. Sometimes the answers are found, but often they are not. Glen would have benefited from knowing that his father had committed suicide because he, too, could not forgive himself, and he thought suicide was the only way out.

Friend, there is hope. If your life has been marred by murder in any form, remember the Apostle Paul. He described himself as the "chief sinner," because he had done everything he could to persecute and put to death anyone who followed Jesus Christ. In the verses below, Christ's followers are referred to as "this way," or, "the way."

And Saul, yet breathing out threatenings and slaughter against the disciples of the Lord, went unto the high priest, And desired of him letters to Damascus to the synagogues, that if he found any of this way, whether they were men or women, he might bring them bound unto Jerusalem. Acts 9:1-2

And I persecuted this way unto the death, binding and delivering into prisons both men and women. Acts 22:4

Saul, who later became the Apostle Paul, hated Christians so much that he handed them over to be executed.

Whosoever hateth his brother is a murderer: and ye know that no murderer hath eternal life abiding in him. 1 John 3:15

Yet, Paul was able to receive God's forgiveness, and to forgive himself.

And I thank Christ Jesus our Lord, who hath enabled me, for that he counted me faithful, putting me into the ministry; Who was before a blasphemer, and a persecutor, and injurious: but I obtained mercy, because I did it ignorantly in unbelief. And the grace of our Lord was exceeding abundant with faith and love which is in Christ Jesus. This is a faithful saying, and worthy of all acceptation, that Christ Jesus came into the world to save sinners; of whom I am chief. Howbeit for this cause I obtained mercy, that in me first Jesus Christ might shew forth all longsuffering, for a pattern to them which should hereafter believe on him to life everlasting. Now unto the King eternal, immortal, invisible, the only wise God, be honour and glory for ever and ever. Amen. 1 Timothy 1:12-17

What can be worse than murder? Refusing to forgive yourself for committing murder.

Janie and the Apostle Paul were able to forgive themselves, be set free, and begin new, glorious lives in Christ. Andy was not. Glen lived his life blaming himself for his father's suicide, and, like Andy, spent his life bitter, critical of others, and consumed with guilt.

Murder is not unforgiveable! Don't listen to the lies of the devil. Remember, he is a liar from the beginning, and he is the father of lies. He is the accuser of the brethren.

For the accuser of our brethren is cast down, which accused them before our God day and night. Revelation 12:10b

Yes, God can forgive even the sin of murder. Turn to Him in repentance, and ask Him to forgive you. He will. Then, forgive yourself, be set free, and live.

Chapter 2: Rape

A sordid and disturbing story of rape is recorded in 2 Samuel 13. The king of Israel, King David, had multiple sons and daughters by several wives and concubines. Absalom and Tamar, two of his children, were full-blooded brother and sister, and Amnon was their half-brother. Amnon lusted after his half-sister, Tamar, and devised a plot to sleep with her. He pretended he was sick, and asked Tamar to bring him some food.

So Tamar went to her brother Amnon's house; and he was laid down. And she took flour, and kneaded it, and made cakes in his sight, and did bake the cakes. And she took a pan, and poured them out before him; but he refused to eat. And Amnon said, Have out all men from me. And they went out every man from him. And Amnon said unto Tamar, Bring the meat into the chamber, that I may eat of thine hand. And Tamar took the cakes which she had made, and brought them into the chamber to Amnon her brother. And when she had brought them unto him to eat, he took hold of her, and said unto her, Come lie with me, my sister. And she answered him, Nay, my brother, do not force me; for no such thing ought to be done in Israel: do not thou this folly. And I, whither shall I cause my shame to go? and as for thee, thou shalt be as one of the fools in Israel. Now therefore, I pray thee, speak unto the king; for he will not withhold me from thee. Howbeit he would not hearken unto her voice: but, being stronger than she, forced her, and lay with her. Then Amnon hated her exceedingly; so that the hatred wherewith he hated her was greater than the love wherewith he had loved her. And Amnon said unto her, Arise, be gone. And she said unto him, There is no cause: this evil in sending me away is greater than the other that thou didst unto me. But he would not hearken unto her. Then he called his servant that ministered unto him, and said, Put now this woman out from me, and bolt the door after her. And she had a garment of divers colours upon her: for with such robes were the king's daughters that were virgins apparelled. Then his servant brought her out, and bolted the door after her. And Tamar put ashes on her head, and rent her garment of divers colours that was on her, and laid her hand on her head, and went on crying. 2 Samuel 13:8-19

The Bible says that Absolom hated his brother Amnon for raping their sister. He plotted to kill him, and succeeded two years later.

We cannot be sure of the long-term effects that the rape had on Tamar. After this incident, she is not mentioned again in scripture. But most rape victims blame themselves. It's entirely possible that Tamar rehearsed the scenario in her mind, over and over. "Why did I go there? I should have taken someone with me. I should have known better. I should have suspected that something wasn't right."

***

Jackie was raped by someone she loved and trusted. She loved him so much, in fact, that she tried to convince herself that it wasn't really rape. After all, she hadn't been raped at knife point by a stranger in a dark alley. Like most rape victims, she blamed herself for "allowing" herself to be raped. She sank into a deep depression, which was almost like a stupor.

"I said no," she explained, with tears streaming down her face. "But he wouldn't stop. I was crying, but he wouldn't stop. When it was all over, he fell asleep like everything was okay. But it wasn't okay!"

Jackie had a very hard time forgiving herself for the circumstances surrounding the rape. She believed that she was in the wrong place at the wrong time, and that she should have known better and been more alert. But she eventually was able to forgive herself. Being raped is never the victims' fault, as much as they may blame themselves. Eventually, with God's help, she was able to see that and receive healing.

Many young men find themselves in situations that quickly get out of hand. When alcohol is involved, these situations can go from bad to worse.

Mike was at a party with a lot of other people. It was a chaotic scene, with loud music, loud conversations, and lots of alcohol. He noticed several young men slip out of the room into an adjoining bedroom, and out of curiosity, he decided to join them. He was surprised to see Laura, a classmate, passed out drunk on the bed, with two of the boys undressing her. Everyone was laughing.

By this time Mike had had a lot to drink. Somewhere in the back of his mind, he knew that everything about this situation was horribly wrong. But alcohol and mob mentality won out. Laura, unconscious, was gang raped that night, and Mike was just one of the gang.

On Monday, in school, there was a lot of whispering and finger-pointing. Among the boys who had participated in raping Laura, there was a lot of bragging. For Mike, there was devastation.

Like many people who are unable to forgive themselves, Mike's life spiraled downward after that point. He began drinking heavily, using drugs, and cutting classes. The summer after his senior class graduated, he hanged himself.

Raping another person cuts to the very heart of what we believe about privacy, decency, human rights, and the beauty of the sex act, as God intended it to be used.

In Judges 19, we read another sordid and horrifying story of rape. A man was traveling back to his home, having visited his concubine at her father's home. She came with him on the way back, and they stopped at an old man's house, who offered to put them up for the night. During the night, some men of the city beat on the old man's door, and demanded that he produce the man who was staying with him (not the woman), because they wanted to have sex with him. The old man refused, instead offering the man's concubine to them as a substitute, and the younger man agreed to this. The Bible records the horrifying account:

But the men would not hearken to him: so the man took his concubine, and brought her forth unto them; and they knew her, and abused her all the night until the morning: and when the day began to spring, they let her go. Then came the woman in the dawning of the day, and fell down at the door of the man's house where her lord was, till it was light. And her lord rose up in the morning, and opened the doors of the house, and went out to go his way: and, behold, the woman his concubine was fallen down at the door of the house, and her hands were upon the threshold. And he said unto her, Up, and let us be going. But none answered. Then the man took her up upon an ass, and the man rose up, and gat him unto his place. And when he was come into his house, he took a knife, and laid hold on his concubine, and divided her, together with her bones, into twelve pieces, and sent her into all the coasts of Israel. And it was so, that all that saw it said, There was no such deed done nor seen from the day that the children of Israel came up out of the land of Egypt unto this day: consider of it, take advice, and speak your minds. Judges 19:25-30

After being raped all night long, this poor woman crawled back to the place where she was staying, and died on the doorstep.

Reading between the lines of scripture, I have to conclude that her lover (referred to as "her lord") could not forgive himself for offering her to the men of the city to be used as a sex slave for the night. Knowing that he was the one they really wanted, and knowing that he had used her to save his own skin, he must have been overcome with grief and remorse. I believe a certain madness must have overtaken him, prompting him to cut her dead body into pieces and send the pieces off to all the coasts of Israel.

Refusing to forgive oneself often results in madness.

You have a choice. If you have been raped, you must decide, here and now, that it was not your fault. Forgive yourself, now, for any blame you have placed on yourself for being raped.

If you have raped someone, you must repent of your actions and ask God to forgive you. He can and He will. Then, forgive yourself. If it is possible, ask the person that you raped to forgive you. I say, if it is possible, because in many instances, for you to come back in contact with your victim would cause her more trauma and more pain, and you don't want to do that. Just know that if you are sorry for what you have done and you have asked for forgiveness, God has indeed forgiven you, and you must forgive yourself. Leave the rest in His hands.

Chapter 3: Adultery

Jesus went unto the mount of Olives. And early in the morning he came again into the temple, and all the people came unto him; and he sat down, and taught them. And the scribes and Pharisees brought unto him a woman taken in adultery; and when they had set her in the midst, They say unto him, Master, this woman was taken in adultery, in the very act. Now Moses in the law commanded us, that such should be stoned: but what sayest thou? This they said, tempting him, that they might have to accuse him. But Jesus stooped down, and with his finger wrote on the ground, as though he heard them not. So when they continued asking him, he lifted up himself, and said unto them, He that is without sin among you, let him first cast a stone at her. And again he stooped down, and wrote on the ground. And they which heard it, being convicted by their own conscience, went out one by one, beginning at the eldest, even unto the last: and Jesus was left alone, and the woman standing in the midst. When Jesus had lifted up himself, and saw none but the woman, he said unto her, Woman, where are those thine accusers? hath no man condemned thee? She said, No man, Lord. And Jesus said unto her, Neither do I condemn thee: go, and sin no more. John 8:1 - 11

I believe this woman was able to forgive herself. Coming within a hair's breadth of being stoned to death, and being miraculously rescued from that, then seeing the love and acceptance in Jesus' eyes, I think she had no choice but to forgive herself. Like so many Bible characters, she passed into and out of the narrative in one account, so there is no way to say for sure.

But Lana was not able to forgive herself. She had been bored with her marriage, bored with her life, and bored with her husband most of all. He was a "regular Joe" who wasn't very exciting. He was self-employed, and didn't make enough money to suit her. He also preferred staying home on Friday night, instead of taking her out on the town, which is what she wanted.

When Lana met John, sparks flew. He was everything her husband was not. Before long, they began a secret adulterous relationship.

Of course, her husband found out. He confronted Lana, and to his shock and hurt, she demanded a divorce. She was going to marry John, she said, and her life would be a whole lot better.

So, Lana divorced her husband, married John, and dragged her three young children into his house. But it didn't take long for her and John to begin arguing – about the children, about money, and about pretty much anything.

Having been through one divorce already, and surviving it, Lana thought nothing much about divorcing John. But this time, the loneliness she felt was different. She also was forced to see, for the first time, the devastating effects that leaving her first husband had had on their children. They suffered nightmares, and clung to her when they were out in public.

One day, it all came crashing down on Lana. She looked around at the dumpy apartment she was living in. She was exhausted from working two jobs, and the children were acting up. She knew what she had to do.

With tears streaming down her face, she paid a visit to her first husband. She told him how sorry she was for leaving him, for hurting him and their children, and for the terrible mess she had made of their lives. She begged him to forgive her and take her back. But instead of forgiveness, Lana received scorn and contempt. Her first husband, still terribly hurt by what she had done to their family, was not about to surrender his pride and forgive her. He threw her out and told her not to come back.

Lana, in dire emotional and economic straits, quickly married again. She then divorced again. The last I knew, she was living with her fifth husband. Her children are grown and scattered. She is a sad and lonely person, one who has never been able to forgive herself.

Too often, we make the mistake of basing our actions on what other people are doing or saying. Our modern culture feeds into this. We are all told that if we're not happy, we need to do whatever it takes to get happy, even if it means breaking up our family. Lana's first mistake was leaving her husband. When things didn't work out as she had hoped, she fell into a downward spiral of mistakes. Panicked by a life spinning out of control, she couldn't put the brakes on long enough to take stock and reevaluate her situation.

King David is another example of a person whose life was out of control. We read the account of the adultery he committed with Bathsheba in 2 Samuel 11 - 12. After committing adultery, he resorted to murdering his lover's husband, Uriah. If Uriah was dead, he reasoned, there could be no jealous husband to confront him when it became obvious that Bathsheba was carrying the king's child.

King David's life quickly went from bad to worse. First adultery, then murder, then the death of his beloved child.

After over a year of hiding and lying, David was confronted by the prophet Nathan. He was warned that because of his actions, his child was about to die. David cried out to the Lord in repentance.

David therefore besought God for the child; and David fasted, and went in, and lay all night upon the earth. And the elders of his house arose, and went to him, to raise him up from the earth: but he would not, neither did he eat bread with them. And it came to pass on the seventh day, that the child died. And the servants of David feared to tell him that the child was dead: for they said, Behold, while the child was yet alive, we spake unto him, and he would not hearken unto our voice: how will he then vex himself, if we tell him that the child is dead? But when David saw that his servants whispered, David perceived that the child was dead: therefore David said unto his servants, Is the child dead? And they said, He is dead. Then David arose from the earth, and washed, and anointed himself, and changed his apparel, and came into the house of the LORD, and worshipped: then he came to his own house; and when he required, they set bread before him, and he did eat. Then said his servants unto him, What thing is this that thou hast done? thou didst fast and weep for the child, while it was alive; but when the child was dead, thou didst rise and eat bread. And he said, While the child was yet alive, I fasted and wept: for I said, Who can tell whether GOD will be gracious to me, that the child may live? But now he is dead, wherefore should I fast? can I bring him back again? I shall go to him, but he shall not return to me. 2 Samuel 12:16 – 23

This is truly one of the saddest stories in the Bible. It is also one of the greatest redemption stories.

David, a musician and songwriter, wrote one of the most beautiful Psalms known to man, Psalm 51. In it, he admits his sin, asks God to forgive him, reminds himself of God's mercy and grace to those who are undeserving of it (all of us), and asks God to wash him clean once again.

David was finally able to forgive himself. The second son born to him with Bathsheba later became King Solomon, the wisest man who ever lived.

Satan will always try to pressure us into making quick decisions, especially when we are under great emotional or financial stress. Remember this: God is willing and able to forgive adultery, even if your spouse is not. If you have fallen into this sin, repent, turn around, and like the woman in the temple, go and sin no more. If you resolve to live your life for Him from now on, He will give you the power to forgive yourself and to find new rest and peace in Him.

Forgive yourself.

Chapter 4: Incest and pedophilia

Sodom was a very wicked city. God destroyed it with fire and brimstone which fell from the sky, and burned it to ashes. But God, in His mercy, warned a man named Lot, who lived in Sodom, that he needed to get out. At the last possible moment, Lot and his two daughters fled the city and took refuge in a cave in a mountain.

And Lot went up out of Zoar, and dwelt in the mountain, and his two daughters with him; for he feared to dwell in Zoar: and he dwelt in a cave, he and his two daughters. And the firstborn said unto the younger, Our father is old, and there is not a man in the earth to come in unto us after the manner of all the earth: Come, let us make our father drink wine, and we will lie with him, that we may preserve seed of our father. And they made their father drink wine that night: and the firstborn went in, and lay with her father; and he perceived not when she lay down, nor when she arose. And it came to pass on the morrow, that the firstborn said unto the younger, Behold, I lay yesternight with my father: let us make him drink wine this night also; and go thou in, and lie with him, that we may preserve seed of our father. And they made their father drink wine that night also: and the younger arose, and lay with him; and he perceived not when she lay down, nor when she arose. Thus were both the daughters of Lot with child by their father. Genesis 19:30 - 36

I wonder how Lot felt when he sobered up, and realized that both of his daughters were pregnant by him. The scripture doesn't tell us – nor does it tell us if either of his daughters ever felt remorse for their shocking sin of incest.

***

Danny was a man who was plunged into marriage at an early age, due to his girlfriend's unexpected pregnancy. His two daughters were born very close together. Danny felt overwhelmed by the demands of marriage and fatherhood. His own father had been distant and demanding, and like too many young men, Danny didn't have a godly example of fatherhood to follow.

Danny had never been a ladies' man. He didn't know what it meant to be a good husband. And, his new wife was always busy with the baby girls, and not really attuned to his needs.

The incest started out innocently enough. Danny would touch his girls inappropriately while bathing them or changing their diapers. At first, he reasoned that what he was doing wasn't really wrong – after all, he loved his daughters, and touching them was just his way of showing them that he loved them.

Danny's wife was a bit flighty. She didn't know what he was doing to their daughters in secret. All she knew was that she was tired of being stuck at home with two young children, and she soon left him to look for excitement elsewhere. Fortunately for the girls, she took them with her.

The breakup of his marriage was devastating to Danny, but he was forced to admit that it was best for his children. Try as he might, he had been unable to keep his hands off of them. He had come to the conclusion that his actions were wrong, but he didn't know how to stop.

The shadow of pedophilia dogged Danny for the rest of his life. Although he remarried, he remained attracted to little girls. He eventually received Jesus Christ as his Savior, but the church he attended was extremely legalistic and Calvinist. He always felt that he had to do more and more good deeds in order to outweigh his evil deeds of molesting his own children. Even worse, he wasn't ready to fully let go of his sin. Although born again, he refused to get baptized, because he felt that if he did, he would then have to "really" give up pedophilia. His second and third wives also eventually left him. He ended up living a reclusive, lonely life, unable to forgive himself.

Annie was molested during her childhood several times – once by her own brother. Each time, she told her mother. Each time, her mother failed to act to protect her. But Annie was blessed with a strong relationship with Christ from an early age. Unlike many victims of sexual abuse, she never blamed herself for it, so she never had to forgive herself. She was also able to forgive her abusers.

It's interesting how pedophiles are regarded within the prison system. In the world of those incarcerated, child molesters are the worst of the worst – far below murderers and rapists.

How does God view incest and pedophilia?

But whoso shall offend one of these little ones which believe in me, it were better for him that a millstone were hanged about his neck, and that he were drowned in the depth of the sea. Matthew 18:6

Take heed that ye despise not one of these little ones; for I say unto you, That in heaven their angels do always behold the face of my Father which is in heaven. Matthew 18:10

None of you shall approach to any that is near of kin to him, to uncover their nakedness: I am the LORD. Leviticus 18:6

Incest and pedophilia are very damaging to those who are its victims. As with all types of sexual assault, these acts are never the victims' fault.

If you are the perpetrator, God stands ready, willing, and able to forgive you for the sins of incest and pedophilia. Once He has forgiven you, you must forgive yourself.

Incest and pedophilia are demonic strongholds. If you are unable to break free from these sins, you need to seek deliverance from a proven deliverance ministry. It is not only possible to be delivered from these sins, it is easy for God to do.

Behold, I am the LORD, the God of all flesh: is there any thing too hard for me? Jeremiah 32:27

If the Son therefore shall make you free, ye shall be free indeed. John 8:36

Chapter 5: Fornication

Fornication is an old-fashioned word that is rarely used these days, except in Christian circles. It means sexual contact before marriage.

Even among Christians, fornication is something that is usually brushed off as being not that important. But the Bible says differently:

Flee fornication. Every sin that a man doeth is without the body; but he that committeth fornication sinneth against his own body. What? know ye not that your body is the temple of the Holy Ghost which is in you, which ye have of God, and ye are not your own? For ye are bought with a price: therefore glorify God in your body, and in your spirit, which are God's. 1 Corinthians 6:18-20

Since fornication is so common, we tend to minimize the seriousness of it. But fornication does have long-term consequences.

When my son was entering his teen years, I decided to have a serious talk with him. I like to use visual aids, so I got a pad of adhesive notes and pulled one off. "You see this little sticky note?" I asked him. "That represents you." I pulled another one off. "You see this one? It represents a girl that you have physical contact with." I stuck the two notes together. "You are stuck to her like glue. But then, you break up." I pulled one of the notes off of the other one and threw it on the floor. "But here comes another girl." I stuck another note to the first note. "You have physical contact with her as well. But then, you break up with her also." I threw the note on the

23

floor. I grabbed another one. "This cycle keeps repeating itself, until one day you meet the young woman you want to marry. But now there is a problem. You have lost your "stickiness," since you have stuck yourself to so many other people. The Bible says: 'Therefore shall a man leave his father and his mother, and shall cleave unto his wife: and they shall be one flesh' (Genesis 2:24). How can you cleave (cling to) your wife, if you've clung to so many other people before you met her? You will have a tough time."

I would love to say that my son eagerly welcomed this unsolicited parental advice. I think the only reaction I got from him was an eye roll.

I hope he took it to heart.

When you look at the consequences of fornication in your life or someone else's, look at it from God's viewpoint. God's very best plan is for you and me to have one sexual partner in our lifetime, and one marriage. If everyone on this planet adhered to that rule, there would be no sexually transmitted diseases, no out of wedlock pregnancies, and no hindrance in cleaving or clinging to our spouses. Nothing good comes of fornication, just like nothing good comes of any sin. No matter how much two people love each other, or think they love each other, when fornication occurs and the relationship ends, it ends with two broken-hearted people. You have given your body, which is to be reserved exclusively for your spouse, to someone who is not your spouse. When we break God's laws, we are the ones who end up broken. This is why the Bible tells us to "flee" fornication. Literally, you need to run for your life from this very common sin.

Remember that God invented sex; human beings did not. He created it, so that means it is beautiful. But it is beautiful only when it is used as God intended it to be used. When it is misused, it becomes an ugly sin.

Sexual contact before marriage is sin.

Many people think this is an old-fashioned rule for another time, and it doesn't apply today. Oh, really? When I was a teenager, one in sixteen people had a sexually transmitted disease. Today that statistic is one in five.

Someone is objecting: "How can I realistically avoid fornication? I'm human, after all. How am I supposed to resist it?"

Many people put themselves in completely avoidable situations, and then they feel that they are unable to escape. If you want to avoid fornication, don't put yourself in a situation where it has any possibility of occurring. For example, I make it a practice to never be alone with a man. When I meet a male friend for dinner or coffee, it is always in a public place. If I invite people over to my house, I always make sure I invite several males and females. One of my female friends remains until the last person has left. By following these simple rules, fornication can never occur.

Many years ago, I heard a Christian man who was attracted to other men complaining sadly about being celibate. His main issue was that the rest of us could remain celibate until we found our mates, but he would have to be celibate for the rest of his life. This man loved Jesus; he just happened to struggle with same-sex attraction. He was also wise enough to realize that a same-sex physical union was sin in God's eyes.

Fornication is sin, whether it is occurs with the same or the opposite sex. And the same rules apply on both sides. The person who struggles with same-sex attraction must make sure that he is never alone with someone of the same sex.

It certainly is discouraging to believe that you have to remain celibate for the rest of your life. It is like the alcoholic who says to himself, "I can never take another drink for the rest of my life."

Praise God; our good Lord did not design our lives to be lived all at once – "the rest of my life" - today. He designed our lives to be lived one day at a time.

Take therefore no thought for the morrow: for the morrow shall take thought for the things of itself. Sufficient unto the day is the evil thereof. Matthew 6:34

Tell yourself the truth. Say, "Today I am dedicating myself to the Lord. I will be celibate, today, for His glory."

If you say, "I have to be celibate for the rest of my life," you will either become mired in depression, or you will hang yourself.

We all have to step back from our current situations and take the long view – God's view.

The wife hath not power of her own body, but the husband: and likewise also the husband hath not power of his own body, but the wife. 1 Corinthians 7:4

Even if you are unmarried, you do not have power over your own body! This was a beautiful revelation from God to me. My husband, before he appears in my life, and wherever he may happen to be, has power over my body. When you think about the long view, think about your future mate. What do you want him/her to be doing right now? Do you want that person to be messing around physically with someone else? I think not.

Is celibacy an easy way to live? No. But committing fornication always adds more heartache to your life and mine, and makes it much harder to cling to your true mate, when he or she comes along.

For the man with same-sex attraction mentioned previously, the choice to remain celibate and serve God as a celibate believer may not seem like a joyful thing, but I can say with absolute certainty, it is the very best choice.

For there are some eunuchs, which were so born from their mother's womb: and there are some eunuchs, which were made eunuchs of men: and there be eunuchs, which have made themselves eunuchs for the kingdom of heaven's sake. He that is able to receive it, let him receive it. Matthew 19:12

The word "eunuch" is another old-fashioned word that is not used much today. In biblical times, a eunuch was a man who had been castrated. Eunuchs "born from their mother's womb" means that there are some people –

admittedly a small group – who have no desire to have a physical relationship with another person. A eunuch "made by man" is self-explanatory. Eunuchs who have made themselves eunuchs for the kingdom of heaven's sake should include every unmarried Christian person. God gives us the grace to be a eunuch for a temporary season in life, until He brings us the right mate, and if that doesn't happen, He gives us the grace to remain an unmarried eunuch until we go home to be with the Lord.

Remember: live your life one day at a time. Dedicate your body to the Lord today. He knows what is best for you, and He has a wonderful plan for you.

***

Max was a hard drinker and a hard partyer. At a party one night, after drinking for hours, he had a homosexual encounter with another drunken party-goer. As is usually the case when one is drunk, he didn't fully understand what had happened until the next day.

By the grace of God, Max was able to step back from the situation and look at it through God's eyes. He recognized that he had sinned, asked God to forgive him, and was able to let go of the incident and forgive himself. He believes that God used this encounter to sober him up, literally. After that night, Max never touched alcohol again, and never had another sexual encounter with a man.

I heard a wonderful preacher on the radio say this: "Ask God to fix your wanter." In other words, ask God to remove from you the things that you want that are not pleasing to Him, and replace them with things that are pleasing to Him.

If your life has been marred by fornication, there is good news for you. You can decide, today, that you will begin again as a spiritual virgin, if not a physical one.

It is of the LORD's mercies that we are not consumed, because his compassions fail not. They are new every morning: great is thy faithfulness. Lamentations 3:22 – 23

If God's mercies are new every morning, and they are, that means that today, this very day, you can ask Him to forgive you, forgive yourself, and begin a new, celibate life.

Like every other sin we commit, we must forgive ourselves for fornication. Forgive yourself, wash yourself in the blood of Jesus Christ, and you will be cleansed.

And to her was granted that she should be arrayed in fine linen, clean and white: for the fine linen is the righteousness of saints. Revelation 19:8

Chapter 6: Marriage and divorce

Did you marry the wrong person? Or,

Do you regret your divorce?

It is certainly very sad that divorce statistics among believers are not that much different than those of non-believers. It is sad, but it is true.

The Bible is replete with examples of unhappy marriages.

In 2 Samuel 6:16, we read about King David dancing joyfully when the ark of the covenant was returned to Israel, and his wife Michel watching him through the window, and despising him.

In Esther 1:12, we read that Queen Vashti refused to present herself before her husband, King Ahasuerus, which infuriated him. Vashti "disappeared" after this incident.

In 1 Samuel 25:25, we have an example of a wife referring to her husband as a fool.

And, these are just a few examples! There are many more.

***

Ashley waited a long time to get married. As a Christian who truly loved Jesus, she wanted to wait for the right man to come along. The years turned into decades, and she began to despair that it would ever happen.

As any single person can attest, the loneliness of the unmarried can be almost unbearable at times.

Then, Ashley met Derek. She wasn't alone anymore! He asked her to marry him, and she said yes. But there was one problem. Derek was not a believer.

Ashley knew that the Bible warns against Christians marrying non-Christians, but the loneliness of her life had overwhelmed her. They got married.

Marriage to an unbeliever comes with enormous challenges. Ashley found this out soon enough. Because she loved Jesus so much, she was determined to see it through. Divorce was not an option in her mind. But, the loneliness she had felt as a single person had now been exchanged for the loneliness of being a believer who had nothing in common with her unbelieving husband. When she tried to talk to Derek about Jesus, she was met with silence, or an immediate change of subject. When she was watching a Christian ministry program on TV, Derek would walk into the room, grab the remote, and change the channel.

Ashley went through a time of self-condemnation. She knew she had sinned by marrying Derek, but she also felt that as a Christian, she had no way out. She repented before the Lord with tears, many times.

Isn't our Lord so gracious? He gently enveloped Ashley with His love. He let her know that He still loved her, and He still had a plan for her life. He showed her that

He did not condemn her for her mistake, and that she should not condemn herself, either.

Ashley and Derek are still married, almost twenty years later. She prays for his salvation daily, and she believes that God will reveal Himself to Derek. She has let go of the self-condemnation, and has come to peace with her decision. Like all married couples, believing or not, she and Derek have their ups and downs, but they are still together, and they love one another.

Alex was married to a depressed and neurotic woman. She spent a lot of time crying. Like most men, Alex did not understand his wife's tears, although he made a tremendous effort. After many years, he filed for divorce and almost immediately remarried.

Unfortunately, Alex had gone from the frying pan into the fire. His new wife was very demanding and argumentative. While his previous wife had been soft-spoken and compliant, his new wife was loud and very hard to please. Everything he did was wrong, it seemed. More than once, while his current wife was yelling at him, he caught himself remembering his previous wife's quiet demeanor and gentle answers. To make matters worse, his previous wife had been miraculously delivered from her mental problems and had gone on to make a new, successful life for herself. Alex felt like kicking himself for throwing away his marriage to her.

But Alex was a very prideful man. He knew that he had made a terrible mistake in divorcing his wife. But he refused to repent of that mistake and ask for forgiveness. He was determined to grit his teeth and stick it out with his new wife. She, in turn, was determined to make his life a living hell.

Divorce and remarriage among Christians is a very sensitive subject. It is almost impossible to find a family that has not been somehow affected by divorce. So let's get down to the nitty-gritty.

If you have married the wrong person, it is a sin like any other sin, and it must be repented of. Rest assured, Satan will try to convince you, me, and everyone else that we have married the wrong person, whether or not that is true. Remember, he is a liar.

Examine your heart. Do not listen to the voice of Satan in this matter! Ask God. Deep within your core, you know if you have sinned by marrying the wrong person. If you have met someone who is younger and more attractive than your current mate, this is not "proof" that you have married the wrong person! This is a trap of the enemy.

After spending time in prayer and fasting, if you have realized that you have married the wrong person, you have a decision to make. Ashley chose to give her marriage to God and remain married to her unbelieving spouse. You may choose to leave. But bear in mind, if you have children, they will be emotionally scarred if you divorce. I say this not to condemn anyone; it is a simple fact. God will not impose His will on you or me. He gives us our lives and leaves it up to us as to how we choose to live them. Make the right choice.

Forgive yourself for marrying the wrong person. If you have repented of it, God has also forgiven you.

If you are divorced and you regret it, forgive yourself for that as well. God hates divorce (Malachi 2:16), but you don't have to hate yourself! If possible, go to your former spouse and ask for forgiveness. It may not be possible for you to do that without causing turmoil in his or her life, but do it if you can.

I know of miraculous stories of people who divorced, and God brought them back together again. If this is your desire, ask Him for this. He can do it.

Behold, I am the LORD, the God of all flesh: is there any thing too hard for me? Jeremiah 32:27

Chapter 7: Domestic violence

Violence in the home has been going on since mankind has been on the earth.

And Cain talked with Abel his brother: and it came to pass, when they were in the field, that Cain rose up against Abel his brother, and slew him.   And the LORD said unto Cain, Where is Abel thy brother? And he said, I know not: Am I my brother's keeper? And he said, What hast thou done? the voice of thy brother's blood crieth unto me from the ground. Genesis 4:8 - 10

As we saw in chapter one, Cain did not forgive himself for killing his brother. The Bible doesn't even indicate that he ever repented of it. Whenever we sin, it is much easier to blame someone else than to take responsibility ourselves.

***

Randy had married a woman much younger than he was. She was immature and overly emotional at times. Randy thought that she just needed a good dose of reality, so she could learn what life and marriage were all about.

At first, the abuse was just a slap here and there. Her tears made him uncomfortable, and he justified hitting her by telling himself that if she didn't cry so much, he wouldn't hit her. But as with all abusers, he didn't stop with just a slap. The abuse soon escalated into full-blown physical fights. Randy had always been shorter and smaller than most other men, so it was a new experience for him to actually have the upper hand in a physical fight. His young wife became his punching bag.

The more he beat his wife, the more she cried and begged him to stop. Her begging filled him with contempt for her.

But one day, she didn't beg. She fought back, ferociously. Randy was so taken aback that he stopped hitting her immediately. He was very shaken by the incident. He vowed to himself not to hit her again.

But it was too late. When he came home from work the next day, he found that she had packed her things and left.

Now Randy was the one who was begging. He pleaded with her to come back. He told her that he was a new man and had turned over a new leaf. But his wife had been hit one too many times. She filed for divorce and never came back.

Randy never remarried. He was never able to forgive himself for hitting his wife, a beautiful young girl with so much potential. He is now an old man, living a sad and lonely life.

I am convinced that those who beat their loved ones are suffering from demonic possession. Think about it: Why would you hit the one you love the most?

If you are an abuser, get help from someone who will hold you accountable for your actions. As with incest and pedophilia, physical violence can be a demonic stronghold. Contact a proven deliverance ministry for help in overcoming this stronghold.

God will help you. Turn from your sin, make restitution for what you have done, and then forgive yourself.

The LORD trieth the righteous: but the wicked and him that loveth violence his soul hateth. Psalm 11:5

Chapter 8: Substance abuse and addictions

The Bible is full of examples of drunkenness. Previously, in chapter four, we read the story of Lot. Lot was so drunk that he had sex with his two daughters, impregnating both of them. Many other people we read about in the Bible had a problem with drunkenness.

And Noah began to be an husbandman, and he planted a vineyard: And he drank of the wine, and was drunken; and he was uncovered within his tent. Genesis 9:20 - 21

We don't know if Noah had an ongoing problem with getting drunk, or if this was a one-time situation. Even if it happened only once, it caused a lot of problems.

In Esther chapter one, we read about King Ahasuerus, who had been feasting and drinking for many days.

On the seventh day, when the heart of the king was merry with wine...Esther 1:10a

Ahasuerus wanted his wife to come appear before him and his friends in the midst of his drunken party. She refused.

Ahasuerus, like many of us, made a lot of great plans while he was drunk, and then later, after sobering up, discovered his plans were not so great after all. He was a notorious drinker.

And the king and Haman sat down to drink; but the city Shushan was perplexed. Esther 3:15b

In 1 Samuel 25, we read about Abigail and her husband, Nabal. Nabal, whose name means "fool," imagined himself to be a very important man. The more he drank, the more important he became in his own eyes.

And Abigail came to Nabal; and, behold, he held a feast in his house, like the feast of a king; and Nabal's heart was merry within him, for he was very drunken: wherefore she told him nothing, less or more, until the morning light. 1 Samuel 25:36

Abigail was wise not to try to have a conversation with a drunken man.

***

Don was a hard-working man who also had an alcohol problem. He spent his days doing manual labor, and his evenings drinking beer. His wife couldn't understand why he came home every night and headed straight to the refrigerator for his nightly brews. He barely spoke to her. In her mind, the beer was his mistress – far more important than she was. And in a way, that was true. Like most alcoholics, he lied about his drinking, and lied about the money he spent on booze. He was not a good father to his children, because alcohol was always number one in his life.

Sam was a gutter alcoholic. He would drink until he passed out, sometimes literally in the gutter. Often he would wake up in a pool of his own vomit. He would drink until he experienced blackouts, and found himself in places he didn't remember going to, with people that he didn't know. He couldn't hold a job and had his driver's license taken away. He drank from morning until night, every day, until he was unconscious.

Don and Sam had similar stories, with different outcomes. Don received Jesus Christ as his Savior, and Jesus miraculously removed his desire to drink, instantaneously. By the grace of God, Don was able to forgive himself for the damage his years of drinking and lies had caused to his family.

Sam, also, was able to quit drinking. He became involved in Alcoholics Anonymous, and became one of its biggest supporters. He never misses a meeting, and hasn't had a drink in over thirty years. But Sam doesn't know Jesus. He believes that if he continues to do enough good deeds, he will eventually make up for all the years of drinking, and somehow finally atone for hurting his family and friends. Somehow, when that elusive day comes, he will then be able to fully forgive himself.

There is a lot about drinking in the Bible, but did you know that drug use is also mentioned?

But these two things shall come to thee in a moment in one day, the loss of children, and widowhood: they shall come upon thee in their perfection for the multitude of thy sorceries, and for the great abundance of thine enchantments. Isaiah 47:9

Neither repented they of their murders, nor of their sorceries, nor of their fornication, nor of their thefts. Revelation 9:21

In the New Testament, the Greek word that is translated as sorcery in our English Bible is pharmakeia. Does that word remind you of anything? Of course, it is the root word of our English words pharmacy, pharmaceutical, pharmacological, etc. It means drugs.

It seems that as long as people have been on this earth, they have been drinking and using drugs.

There are multiple addictions besides drugs and alcohol. These days we have people addicted to their own phones. Talk about a sad situation! Some people are addicted to gambling, shopping, overeating – you name it. If you can't give it up and it interferes with your life, it is an addiction.

Social media addiction is a recognized phenomenon by those in the mental health profession. After spending hours on social media, people are depressed, anxious, sad, worried, nervous, and filled with feelings of inadequacy. Why? People post the very best about their lives on social media - the fun birthday party, the jubilant graduation, and the photos of recent weight loss. Tell me: has anyone ever posted a picture of herself with the caption: This is me, now twenty pounds heavier? No! No one does that. So, we look at a fake world online, compare it to our real world IRL (in real life), and become depressed and anxious. It's no wonder.

The addiction comes in when we feel the need to constantly check social media for updates. Maybe if we check often enough, we will see a photo of someone who is heavier than us, or not as attractive, and then we will feel better about ourselves.

For we dare not make ourselves of the number, or compare ourselves with some that commend themselves: but they measuring themselves by themselves, and comparing themselves among themselves, are not wise. 2 Corinthians 10:12

Like all addictions, social media addiction leaves the addict filled with shame and remorse. After wasting hours online, she tells herself that tomorrow she will put her phone away, and spend her day doing productive things.

Thankfully, God can forgive any addiction. Like Don, whose story we read earlier, we can also forgive ourselves.

Each day is a new day with God.

It is of the LORD's mercies that we are not consumed, because his compassions fail not. They are new every morning: great is thy faithfulness. Lamentations 3:22 - 23

No matter how many times you have failed and been overcome by addiction, God's compassion for you does not fail. His mercy is new every morning. Take today – it's all you have anyway – repent of your addiction, ask God to help you, and then forgive yourself.

Chapter 9: Betrayal

Two men betrayed Jesus Christ. One forgave himself; the other did not. We read their stories in Matthew 26 and 27.

Peter answered and said unto him, Though all men shall be offended because of thee, yet will I never be offended. Jesus said unto him, Verily I say unto thee, That this night, before the cock crow, thou shalt deny me thrice. Peter said unto him, Though I should die with thee, yet will I not deny thee. Likewise also said all the disciples.

Now Peter sat without in the palace: and a damsel came unto him, saying, Thou also wast with Jesus of Galilee. But he denied before them all, saying, I know not what thou sayest. And when he was gone out into the porch, another maid saw him, and said unto them that were there, This fellow was also with Jesus of Nazareth. And again he denied with an oath, I do not know the man. And after a while came unto him they that stood by, and said to Peter, Surely thou also art one of them; for thy speech bewrayeth thee. Then began he to curse and to swear, saying, I know not the man. And immediately the cock crew. And Peter remembered the word of Jesus, which said unto him, Before the cock crow, thou shalt deny me thrice. And he went out, and wept bitterly.
Matthew 26: 33 – 35, 69 - 75

When the morning was come, all the chief priests and elders of the people took counsel against Jesus to put him to death: And when they had bound him, they led him away, and delivered him to Pontius Pilate the governor. Then Judas, which had betrayed him, when he saw that he was condemned, repented himself, and

43

brought again the thirty pieces of silver to the chief priests and elders, Saying, I have sinned in that I have betrayed the innocent blood. And they said, What is that to us? see thou to that. And he cast down the pieces of silver in the temple, and departed, and went and hanged himself. Matthew 27: 1 - 5

The Bible says that Peter went out, and wept bitterly. It also says that Judas went out, and hanged himself. Clearly, both men were overwhelmed with sorrow because of what they had done. The Bible doesn't explicitly tell us that Peter forgave himself, but I believe he did. He went on to preach the gospel powerfully, and his preaching brought thousands of people to Christ. Judas never had an opportunity to forgive himself, because his suicide prevented that from happening.

People betray one another for a variety of reasons. In Peter's case, it was fear. In Judas' case, it was greed.

Some pastors I know were the victims of a stunning betrayal. They were contacted by a church in another country and invited to come minister at a conference. They went by faith, across two continents, at great expense. The Lord moved in a mighty way while they were there. One of the people who had invited them acted as their host, and carefully collected the offerings given by the congregation at every service. This money was intended for the visiting pastors.

When it was time to go back home, no sign of the money that had been collected could be found. When they politely asked their host about the offerings, she became angry and indignant, and told them that *they* should pay *her* for the hotel and miscellaneous expenses of their visit. But the amount collected in the offerings was far more than the amount of these bills.

My pastor friends had stepped out in faith to go to this country to minister, and their travel costs had been exorbitant. They did not receive a penny of the offerings given during the conference. This was not only a huge financial loss, it was also very emotionally and physically draining.

Because they are very kind and forgiving people, my friends forgave this woman for her shocking betrayal and theft. But they shouldered the burden of this debt, which they could not afford, for many years.

Did the woman forgive herself? I don't think so. From various events that occurred after this, it seemed obvious that she twisted things around in her own mind in order to portray herself as a victim, not a perpetrator who needed forgiveness. Like many people who refuse to admit to wrong and the need for forgiveness, her life went into a downward spiral after this.

If you have betrayed someone who trusted you, God can help you to make it right. Peter chose to make it right, but Judas chose not to. Be like Peter. Make it right, and then forgive yourself.

Chapter 10: Abandonment

In Acts 15, we read an interesting story of a mutual abandonment. Two friends and coworkers suddenly had a disagreement that they could not resolve, so each abandoned the other.

Paul also and Barnabas continued in Antioch, teaching and preaching the word of the Lord, with many others also. And some days after Paul said unto Barnabas, Let us go again and visit our brethren in every city where we have preached the word of the LORD, and see how they do. And Barnabas determined to take with them John, whose surname was Mark. But Paul thought not good to take him with them, who departed from them from Pamphylia, and went not with them to the work. And the contention was so sharp between them, that they departed asunder one from the other: and so Barnabas took Mark, and sailed unto Cyprus; And Paul chose Silas, and departed, being recommended by the brethren unto the grace of God.
Acts 15:35 - 40

The Bible doesn't tell us if Barnabas forgave himself for abandoning Paul, but Paul did forgive himself for abandoning Barnabas.

I have fought a good fight, I have finished my course, I have kept the faith: Henceforth there is laid up for me a crown of righteousness, which the Lord, the righteous judge, shall give me at that day: and not to me only, but unto all them also that love his appearing. Do thy diligence to come shortly unto me: For Demas hath forsaken me, having loved this present world, and is departed unto Thessalonica; Crescens to Galatia, Titus unto Dalmatia. Only Luke is with me. Take Mark, and bring him with thee: for he is profitable to me for the ministry. 2 Timothy 4:7-11

In these verses, Paul is asking for Mark to come see him. This is the same Mark that he didn't want to take with him before, and that caused Paul to split from Barnabas. We can tell from this passage that Paul forgave himself and is at peace - ready to go home to be with the Lord.

***

Amy abandoned her husband and her son. She had struggled with depression all of her life, and in the throes of a particularly bad depressive episode, she decided to leave. Of course, this did nothing to improve her situation. Crippled by depression, she was unable to explain to them what she was going through, or why she left.

Her son, who had been a happy-go-lucky child who did well in school, gradually became withdrawn and silent. Her husband, although he tried his best to understand her, eventually became enraged at her behavior.

The Lord miraculously intervened in Amy's life. He lifted her out of depression, and enabled her to forgive herself for breaking up her family. Her life took a different path, and the Lord opened doors to her that she never could have imagined before.

If you have been abandoned, your natural tendency is to blame yourself for this. You ask what you could have done differently to prevent him/her/them from abandoning you. But being abandoned is not your fault!

Can a woman forget her sucking child, that she should not have compassion on the son of her womb? yea, they may forget, yet will I not forget thee. Isaiah 49:15

When my father and my mother forsake me, then the LORD will take me up. Psalm 27:10

Decide in your heart, right now, that you are not to be blamed for being abandoned. Know that God loves you, and He will never abandon you.

If you have abandoned someone who needed you, there is still hope. Asking for forgiveness is always the first step. Whether he or she forgives you or not, forgive yourself. If the person you abandoned is no longer living, ask the Lord to forgive you, and then forgive yourself.

And the peace of God, which passeth all understanding, shall keep your hearts and minds through Christ Jesus. Philippians 4:7

Chapter 11: Stealing

And Laban went to shear his sheep: and Rachel had stolen the images that were her father's. Now Rachel had taken the images, and put them in the camel's furniture, and sat upon them. And Laban searched all the tent, but found them not. And she said to her father, Let it not displease my lord that I cannot rise up before thee; for the custom of women is upon me. And he searched but found not the images. Genesis 31:19, 34 - 35

If you have ever stolen something, you know the guilty conscience that results from stealing. Some of us remember stealing our classmate's purple crayon, back in kindergarten. Some of us have stolen things of much greater value.

In the biblical account above, Rachel and her husband Jacob, her sister, their maids, their children, and their servants had all left Laban's household and were heading back to where Jacob's relatives were. When they were packing everything up for their journey, Rachel also packed the carved false gods that belonged to her father and took them with her. She was clearly guilty, but did not admit it

We don't know why Rachel stole the gods. The Bible doesn't tell us what they were made of. If they were gold or silver, it's possible that she took them solely because of their monetary value. Maybe she stole them because she wanted to worship them, as her father had done. Maybe she took them simply to spite him. But in any case, she took them.

Her husband, Jacob, was quite convinced that no one in his entourage had taken Laban's property. But not too long after Laban searched in vain for his gods, and left to go back home, things changed.

Then Jacob said unto his household, and to all that were with him, Put away the strange gods that are among you, and be clean, and change your garments: And they gave unto Jacob all the strange gods which were in their hand, and all their earrings which were in their ears; and Jacob hid them under the oak which was by Shechem. Genesis 32:2, 4

Somehow Jacob got wind that there were false gods among the people that were with him. It's possible that Rachel had confessed to him what she had done. The fact that she willing gave him the gods leads me to believe that God was dealing with her heart, and convicting her of her sin. Conviction is the first step on the road to self-forgiveness.

We will remain ignorant as to whether Rachel really did forgive herself for being a thief, as the Bible doesn't tell us. Ideally, she should have returned the items she stole. Perhaps she didn't, because she didn't want her father involved in idol worship. That is mere speculation on my part.

I am reminded of an incident that occurred in my own life. It is almost comical to think of it now, but it is a reminder of how easy it is to justify stealing.

Years ago, I had just come home from work, and happened to glance across the street at my neighbor's house. To my shock, a Confederate flag was flying from their flagpole. I was stunned, angry, offended, and disgusted by it. I stomped into the house and immediately started ranting to my roommate, a beautiful young black girl.

"Did you see that flag across the street?" I demanded. She seemed a little startled, probably because of the intensity with which I confronted her.

"Yeah, I think so," she said cautiously. "You mean, the Confederate flag?"

"Yes, the Confederate flag! I can't believe those people would put up a flag like that! That is absolutely disgusting! How can they do that? I'm going to sneak over there in the middle of the night and take that flag down!" I ranted.

She looked at me calmly, with a mixture of amusement and pity on her face.

"Sister Julie," she said soothingly. "That would be stealing."

As quickly as my anger had flared up, it died down. I felt as though she had poured cold water on my hot emotions. I was suddenly embarrassed. Here I was, an older and "more mature" Christian, who should have been the one setting a good example for this younger woman. Instead, I was telling her that I was plotting theft and revenge against my neighbor. I slunk off like a dog with its tail between its legs.

I could have taken the flag down and burned it (which is what I really wanted to do), justifying my actions by telling myself that my neighbors were racist – therefore it was okay to steal from them. Instead, I received a lesson in patience and forgiveness, which I badly needed. I know, if I had gone through with my plan, my conscience would have tormented me to no end, and eventually I would have had to go to my neighbors, admit what I had done, and ask them to forgive me. I would have also had to replace the stolen item! Can you imagine a born-again believer being forced to buy a Confederate flag? Try explaining that situation to anyone.

I am thankful that God used my very wise roommate to spare me the consequences of my impulsive plot.

At a conference recently, I heard a very sobering account of a major theft that occurred in my home state. A woman with a gambling addiction embezzled thousands of dollars from her employer. She had been in a trusted position with them for many years. She embezzled over a long period of time, and gambled away the money that she stole. Of course, she was eventually caught. She is now in prison.

This woman repented with tears, and eventually forgave herself. Her former employer forgave her, too. Unfortunately, the company she had worked for was forced to close, due to the huge monetary loss it had suffered.

When your actions have caused terrible consequences in another person's life, it can be very hard to forgive yourself. But it is very necessary.

By all means, if you are able to make restitution for what you have stolen, do that as soon as you can. Of course, ask the person you have stolen from to forgive you. Remember, the thief on the cross was forgiven by Jesus (Luke 23:43).

You can and must forgive yourself for being a thief in the past. The past is past.

Let him that stole steal no more: but rather let him labour, working with his hands the thing which is good, that he may have to give to him that needeth. Ephesians 4:28

Chapter 12: Lying

And Rebekah spake unto Jacob her son, saying, Behold, I heard thy father speak unto Esau thy brother, saying, Bring me venison, and make me savoury meat, that I may eat, and bless thee before the LORD before my death. Now therefore, my son, obey my voice according to that which I command thee. Go now to the flock, and fetch me from thence two good kids of the goats; and I will make them savoury meat for thy father, such as he loveth: And thou shalt bring it to thy father, that he may eat, and that he may bless thee before his death. And Jacob said to Rebekah his mother, Behold, Esau my brother is a hairy man, and I am a smooth man: My father peradventure will feel me, and I shall seem to him as a deceiver; and I shall bring a curse upon me, and not a blessing. And his mother said unto him, Upon me be thy curse, my son: only obey my voice, and go fetch me them. Genesis 27:6 - 13

Jacob, from the beginning of his life until he was an old man, was a con man, a trickster and a liar. His mother, Rebekah, was no better. We read in this Biblical account of their plot to deceive Jacob's father, Isaac, by Jacob pretending to be Esau, his brother. Jacob got away with his lie – that is, he got what he wanted, a stolen blessing from his father. But as a result of his lie, he ran away from his family and became a fugitive. He never got to see his mother again.   And, he ended up marrying a woman and living with her family, in a household where he was constantly lied to and tricked.

Be not deceived; God is not mocked: for whatsoever a man soweth, that shall he also reap. Galatians 6:7

There are serious consequences for lying. If you are a liar, you can be certain that others will lie to you. It is a guarantee.

Jacob suffered the consequences of his lie for many years. But I do believe he ultimately forgave himself.

After living with his father-in-law's family for many years, he decided to return to his own family. After what he had done to his brother, Esau, he was afraid of him (rightfully so). He sent his wives, children, and servants ahead of him, and he remained behind. I believe this is where he finally came to terms with himself, and faced up to his lifelong habit of lying.

And he rose up that night, and took his two wives, and his two womenservants, and his eleven sons, and passed over the ford Jabbok. And he took them, and sent them over the brook, and sent over that he had. And Jacob was left alone; and there wrestled a man with him until the breaking of the day. And when he saw that he prevailed not against him, he touched the hollow of his thigh; and the hollow of Jacob's thigh was out of joint, as he wrestled with him. And he said, Let me go, for the day breaketh. And he said, I will not let thee go, except thou bless me. And he said unto him, What is thy name? And he said, Jacob. And he said, Thy name shall be called no more Jacob, but Israel: for as a prince hast thou power with God and with men, and hast prevailed. And Jacob asked him, and said, Tell me, I pray thee, thy name. And he said, Wherefore is it that thou dost ask after my name? And he blessed him there. And Jacob called the name of the place Peniel: for I have seen God face to face, and my life is preserved. Genesis 32:22-30

It seems to me that Jacob was terrified of facing his brother Esau. God sent a man to wrestle with him, who Bible scholars believe was a pre-incarnate appearance of Jesus Christ. We can infer that Jacob was not asking for a blessing only. I believe that he was asking for God's forgiveness for his many years of trickery.

And as he passed over Penuel the sun rose upon him, and he halted upon his thigh. Genesis 32:31

Even though Jacob limped for the rest of his life, I believe he received God's forgiveness and forgave himself, as well.

...for I have seen God face to face, and my life is preserved. Genesis 32:30b

There are too many modern-day liars to choose one as an example. The daily news is always full of the latest scandal regarding some politician who lied about something. It's hard to believe that any of these people are sorry for the lies they have told, although I suppose some of them are.

If you have a habit of lying, the first step is to stop lying. The second step is to apologize to those you have lied to. If you are truly sorry for what you have done, you will sincerely apologize, and not use the word "if" in your apology, as in: "If what I said hurt you, I'm sorry."

Anytime you start qualifying your apology, you're not really sorry. And if you're not really sorry, you can never fully forgive yourself for lying, which is the third step.

Parents sometimes lie to their children, and then they are angry when their children lie to them! This is a sensitive subject, but listen to me:

Don't ever tell your child that if he is good, Santa Claus will bring him presents.

Don't ever tell your child that if she puts her tooth under her pillow, the tooth fairy will exchange it for money.

Don't ever tell your child that his dog ran away, when the dog was actually run over by a car.

If you are guilty of any of these lies to your children, ask God to forgive you, and ask your child to forgive you. Then, please, forgive yourself.

This is a very powerful deterrent to lying: When you are tempted to lie, remind yourself that if you do, you will have to go back to the person/people you lied to, admit that you were lying, and ask them to forgive you. This is a very unpleasant experience, and it should stop the lie in its tracks.

If someone is a pathological liar, self-forgiveness is usually not possible without divine intervention. The pathological liar can't tell the difference between the truth and a lie. He lies for no reason, even when telling a lie has no advantage.

My former foster son fits into this category. If he had Cheerios cereal for breakfast, he would tell his teacher that he had Life cereal. If he was wearing a blue shirt, he would tell his biological mother on the phone that he was wearing a red shirt.

Pathological liars live in a world that they have created in their own minds – a world that bears little resemblance to reality. My foster son grew from a lying boy into a lying man. He definitely needs divine intervention in his life. I doubt if he ever realized that he needed to stop lying, apologize, and then forgive himself for lying. I, on the other hand, had to forgive myself for being constantly irritated by his lies.

Lying lips are abomination to the LORD: but they that deal truly are his delight. Proverbs 12:22

Stop lying, apologize, and forgive yourself.

Chapter 13: Gossiping and slandering

But let none of you suffer as a murderer, or as a thief, or as an evildoer, or as a busybody in other men's matters. 1 Peter 4:15

Slander has destroyed more people's lives than murder. Isn't it interesting that in the verse above, God puts gossip (being a busybody) in the same category as murder and theft? You don't need a gun or a knife to murder someone; you can do it with your words.

You shall not go around as a gossip among your people, and you are not to act against the life of your neighbor [with slander or false testimony]; I am the LORD. Leviticus 19:16 (Amplified Bible)

Christian leaders, unfortunately, are the target of a lot of gossip and slander. Some of the true accounts I have heard have literally brought me to tears.

A pastor in another country had a very successful ministry, and other pastors became jealous of him. They paid several young men to say publicly that this pastor had molested them. There was zero truth to this story, but it didn't matter. The pastor's reputation and ministry were destroyed.

That is the profoundly evil and vicious nature of gossip. Even if the gossip proves to be untrue, the victim's name is tarnished forever. In the case above, the pastor was vindicated when the young men confessed to what they had done, but his name will forever be associated with this false scandal.

Closer to home, I know of another case of gossip motivated by jealousy. A pastor and his wife, who were jealous of another pastor's success, literally went house to house in their Christian community and told everyone who would listen that the other pastor had stolen money from an elderly widow in the church. Once again, the story had no basis in fact, but the comments soon started appearing on social media about this "wicked" pastor and his so-called thievery.

I wish that every gossip would stop and think about the damage that his or her words are causing. But they won't, because that is precisely the reason why they are gossiping – they want to cause damage.

When you spread gossip, you almost never know if you have the real story. If you don't know, why repeat it?

Now Absalom had commanded his servants, saying, Mark ye now when Amnon's heart is merry with wine, and when I say unto you, Smite Amnon; then kill him, fear not: have not I commanded you? be courageous, and be valiant. And the servants of Absalom did unto Amnon as Absalom had commanded. Then all the king's sons arose, and every man gat him up upon his mule, and fled. And it came to pass, while they were in the way, that tidings came to David, saying, Absalom hath slain all the king's sons, and there is not one of them left. Then the king arose, and tare his garments, and lay on the earth; and all his servants stood by with their clothes rent. And Jonadab, the son of Shimeah David's brother, answered and said, Let not my lord suppose that they have slain all the young men the king's sons; for Amnon only is dead: for by the appointment of Absalom this hath been determined from the day that he forced his sister

Tamar. Now therefore let not my lord the king take the thing to his heart, to think that all the king's sons are dead: for Amnon only is dead. 2 Samuel 13:28-33

Remember Tamar? We read about her in chapter two. Absalom plotted to kill her rapist, his half-brother Amnon, for two years. After he told his servants to kill Amnon, somehow the story got garbled along the way, as stories usually do, and Amnon's father, King David, was told that all of his sons had been killed by Absalom.

Absalom hath slain all the king's sons, and there is not one of them left. 2 Samuel 13:30b

Some people gossip because they want life to seem more exciting than it actually is. After all, which is more exciting to tell the king: All of your sons are dead, or one of your sons is dead?

In the case of the couple who spread false gossip house-to-house about another pastor, God dealt with them severely. Their marriage began to crumble shortly after this episode, and they are now divorced.

For whom the Lord loveth he chasteneth, and scourgeth every son whom he receiveth. Hebrews 12:6

Don't wait for the Lord to discipline you! If you are a gossip, repent and ask Him to forgive you. Then the difficult task begins. Just as in the case with lying, you need to go to every person that you gossiped to, admit that you were gossiping, and ask each one to forgive you. This may take months, or years. Do it.

And again, just as in the case with lying, if you have to go to every person you gossiped to and gossiped about, apologize, and ask for forgiveness, this is a very strong deterrent against gossiping! It is no fun to have to do this. I know, because I've done it.

When you are finished, you will be able to forgive yourself, and sleep peacefully at night. That is worth more than all the money in the world.

Where no wood is, there the fire goeth out: so where there is no talebearer, the strife ceaseth. Proverbs 26:20

Chapter 14: Barriers to self-forgiveness

And they shall teach no more every man his neighbour, and every man his brother, saying, Know the LORD: for they shall all know me, from the least of them unto the greatest of them, saith the LORD: for I will forgive their iniquity, and I will remember their sin no more. Jeremiah 31:34

Isn't forgiveness the most wonderful thing there is? To know that God forgives me fills me with such awe that I cannot express it.

There are many verses in the Bible about the necessity of forgiveness. I always used to believe that these verses applied to my forgiving of others (and of course, they do). But I never stopped to think about how they apply equally to my forgiveness of myself.

Forgiveness is serious business, and lack of forgiveness is even more serious. The reason why some of us can't forgive ourselves is the same reason why some of us can't forgive others. We believe that they do not deserve forgiveness. I believe that I do not deserve forgiveness.

Then said Jesus, Father, forgive them; for they know not what they do. Luke 23:34a

The people who crucified Jesus did not deserve God's forgiveness. And you and I don't deserve it, either. I force myself to remember this when I am struggling to forgive another person. Forgiveness is not easy!

But if ye do not forgive, neither will your Father which is in heaven forgive your trespasses. Mark 11:26

Because I have sinned so many times, I rush to forgive others who have hurt me. The thought of my heavenly Father not forgiving me is a terrifying thought.

But somehow, refusing to forgive myself doesn't seem as bad as refusing to forgive someone else. In some strange way, refusing to forgive myself almost seems like a holy act.

"You see, God, how angry I am at myself for what I did. That must prove to You how sorry I really am."

I was reading about how some people in bygone eras would literally torture themselves, trying to atone for their sins. They would whip themselves, or wear a shirt made of goat's hair to cause pain and discomfort, as a way of paying for their sins. Today, very few people do these things. Instead, they torture themselves with their own thoughts.

For if we would judge ourselves, we should not be judged. 1 Corinthians 11:31

It's always better to quickly admit your wrongs, rather than have another person point them out to you. The problem arises when we have admitted our wrongs, asked God to forgive us, and then continue to condemn ourselves. Some of us live in self-condemnation every day.

For thou, Lord, art good, and ready to forgive; and plenteous in mercy unto all them that call upon thee. Psalm 86:5

For whosoever shall call upon the name of the Lord shall be saved. Romans 10:13

There is nothing holy about failing to forgive yourself. God sees this as a sin, in the same way He sees failure to forgive others as a sin. If you are trapped in the sin of unforgiveness, the Bible says that you will be saved from this sin, and all other sins, if you call on the name of the Lord.

Sometimes we believe that what we have done is so evil that we simply cannot forgive ourselves. This brings a few questions to mind: If God has forgiven me of all my sins, and I refuse to forgive myself, am I holding myself to a higher standard than God is holding me? Am I saying that it's okay for God to forgive me, but it's not okay for me to forgive myself?

Sometimes we can't forgive ourselves because a particular person (or people) never let us forget about what we have done wrong. Sometimes this is real, and sometimes it's imagined.

After Joseph's brothers sold him into slavery, he became the Vice-Pharoah of Egypt. His life went from being a beloved son to becoming a slave, to being falsely imprisoned, to working in the king's palace. God divinely put him in the right place at the right time in order to rescue his family, and entire countries, from starvation. Yet after all of this, when his father died, his brothers were still consumed by guilt over what they had done to him.

And when Joseph's brethren saw that their father was dead, they said, Joseph will peradventure hate us, and will certainly requite us all the evil which we did unto him. And they sent a messenger unto Joseph, saying, Thy father did command before he died, saying, So shall ye say unto Joseph, Forgive, I pray thee now, the trespass of thy brethren, and their sin; for they did unto thee evil: and now, we pray thee, forgive the trespass of the servants of the God of thy father. And Joseph wept when they spake unto him. And his brethren also went and fell down before his face; and they said, Behold, we be thy servants. And Joseph said unto them, Fear not: for am I in the place of God? But as for you, ye thought evil against me; but God meant it unto good, to bring to pass, as it is this day, to save much people alive. Now therefore fear ye not: I will nourish you, and your little ones. And he comforted them, and spake kindly unto them. Genesis 50:15 - 21

Joseph's brothers were convinced that Joseph would punish them because they sold him into slavery when he was seventeen years old. They were so convinced of this that they made up a story about their father commanding them, before his death, to tell Joseph to forgive them. I think Joseph saw right through this, which is why he wept.

Joseph's brothers lived for years with the guilt and horror of what they had done. They were never able to forgive themselves (although I believe they finally may have done so after Joseph's words to them, above).

Can you imagine living for decades, convinced that the person you wronged is hating you and plotting revenge against you? You would never sleep. In the case of Joseph's brothers, this unforgiveness on Joseph's part was all in their imaginations – it had no basis in reality.

But sometimes, the one we have wronged really won't let us forget. I knew a wife who took great delight in reminding her husband, on every possible occasion, how his stock market investments had failed, and how they had lost a lot of money as a result. She spoke about it openly, with great glee, in front of anyone who would listen, for years and years after the incident occurred. Such constant reminders of our failures can make it very hard to forgive ourselves.

But God forgives.

Who is a God like unto thee, that pardoneth iniquity, and passeth by the transgression of the remnant of his heritage? he retaineth not his anger for ever, because he delighteth in mercy. He will turn again, he will have compassion upon us; he will subdue our iniquities; and thou wilt cast all their sins into the depths of the sea.
Micah 7:18-19

I am not an expert on oceans, but I am fairly sure that no one has ever been to the bottom of the sea. Why? Because the tremendous pressure of the water would crush the person who ventured down there. Imagine your sins on the bottom of the ocean, utterly crushed and pulverized by the water pressure. They have been crushed to dust. There is nothing left of them.

That's how God views your confessed sins. If that's how He sees them, why do you go rooting around on the bottom of the ocean, looking for dust? Doing that will crush you.

Don't do it.

Chapter 15: Consequences of unforgiveness

For if ye forgive men their trespasses, your heavenly Father will also forgive you: But if ye forgive not men their trespasses, neither will your Father forgive your trespasses. Matthew 6: 14 - 15

What could be plainer than that? If I don't forgive, God will not forgive me.

As I have often said, there is no "unforgiven" section in heaven. Everyone there has been forgiven. This underscores the seriousness of unforgiveness.

No doubt, this issue of unforgiveness ignites a theological debate among many people. If salvation is by grace alone, my lack of forgiveness should have nothing to do with my salvation.

Perhaps in our minds it shouldn't, but it does. For the Christian, forgiveness is not optional. Just as we must ask Jesus Christ for His free gift of salvation, we must also ask Him to help us forgive. Jesus died on the cross for all of humanity, so all people, everywhere, could receive salvation and live with Him in heaven for all of eternity. But not everyone is saved. Why not? Because not everyone asks for salvation.

...yet ye have not, because ye ask not. James 4:2b

As my pastor always says, there is soap and water available everywhere, but some people choose not to take a shower.

If you are struggling with unforgiveness, for yourself or someone else, please understand here and now that you must forgive. If there is someone in your life that you can't forgive, you can try to avoid that person, but if you can't forgive yourself, there is nowhere to run.

Unforgiveness has dire consequences. Failing to forgive yourself means that you have despised Jesus' forgiveness of you for your sins. You are saying, in effect, that His forgiveness of you isn't enough, and that His death on the cross was insufficient for your sins.

There is no such thing as a "little" unforgiveness. Like cancer, it grows and grows until you are consumed by it. People who don't forgive, without exception, are bitter, angry, critical, and fault-finding. No one wants to be around such people – they end up alone and friendless.

If you don't forgive yourself, you will be angry and bitter toward yourself. You will criticize yourself and find fault with almost everything you do. You may abuse drugs or alcohol, engage in risky or violent behavior, or eventually commit suicide.

Do you hate yourself?

Hatred always leads to destruction.

But he that hateth his brother is in darkness, and walketh in darkness, and knoweth not whither he goeth, because that darkness hath blinded his eyes. 1 John 2:11

This verse applies to you hating your brother, and it applies equally to you hating yourself. If you hate yourself, the Bible says you are blind and you don't know where you are going.

But I say unto you, Love your enemies, bless them that curse you, do good to them that hate you, and pray for them which despitefully use you, and persecute you...
Matthew 5:44

I had to learn to be good to myself. At one time in my life, it was next to impossible for me to do anything nice for myself, such as buy myself a new pair of shoes, or even get a decent haircut. I always felt that I didn't deserve anything good. Although this verse in Matthew 5 is talking about your relationship with a person who is your enemy, ask yourself this question: Am I my own worst enemy? Too often, we treat ourselves as though we are.

If God warns us against hating another person, don't you think that He doesn't want us to hate ourselves, either?

Every wise woman buildeth her house: but the foolish plucketh it down with her hands. Proverbs 14:1

If you hate yourself, you are literally tearing yourself apart.

God gave you your life, your body, your mind, your soul, your existence, as His gift to you. Don't pluck down your own house (yourself). Don't pick yourself to pieces and tear yourself down. God does not want you to do this to another person, and He doesn't want you to do it to yourself, either.

With the help of my wonderful pastors, I slowly began to see myself as God sees me. He really doesn't see *me* at all; when He looks at me, He sees Jesus Christ. Jesus has washed away all my sins and made me clean. He has dressed me in His white robes of righteousness. That's all that God sees, and that's all that matters. He has forgiven me, and I must forgive myself.

Someone is asking, "How can I forgive myself?" The answer is, the same way you forgive another person.

And one of the Pharisees desired (Jesus) that he would eat with him. And he went into the Pharisee's house, and sat down to meat. And, behold, a woman in the city, which was a sinner, when she knew that Jesus sat at meat in the Pharisee's house, brought an alabaster box of ointment, And stood at his feet behind him weeping, and began to wash his feet with tears, and did wipe them with the hairs of her head, and kissed his feet, and anointed them with the ointment. Now when the Pharisee which had bidden him saw it, he spake within himself, saying, This man, if he were a prophet, would have known who and what manner of woman this is that toucheth him: for she is a sinner. And Jesus answering said unto him, Simon, I have somewhat to say unto thee. And he saith, Master, say on. There was a certain creditor which had two debtors: the one owed five hundred pence, and the other fifty. And when they had nothing to pay, he frankly forgave them both. Tell me therefore, which of them will love him most? Simon answered and said, I suppose that he, to whom he forgave most. And he said unto him, Thou hast rightly judged. And he turned to the woman, and said unto Simon, Seest thou this woman? I entered into thine house, thou gavest me no water for my feet: but she hath washed my feet with tears, and wiped them with the hairs of her head. Thou gavest me no kiss: but this woman since the time I came in hath not ceased to kiss my feet. My head with oil thou didst not anoint: but this woman hath anointed my feet with ointment. Wherefore I say unto thee, Her sins, **which are many***, are forgiven; for she loved much: but to whom little is forgiven, the same loveth little. And he said unto her, Thy sins are forgiven. And they that sat at meat with him began to say within themselves, Who is this that forgiveth sins also? And he said to the woman, Thy faith hath saved thee; go in peace* (bolding added). Luke 7:36 – 50

This is one of my favorite Bible stories. Mary of Bethany, who was Martha and Lazarus' sister (who many Bible scholars believe was the same person as Mary Magdalene), anointed Jesus with fragrant oil as he sat at dinner in Simon's house. The parable that Jesus then told about the creditor and the two debtors is a powerful illustration about the power of forgiveness. Mary loved Jesus, probably more than any other person on earth, because He had forgiven her of many sins, and she recognized the power and the value of that forgiveness.

Failing to forgive yourself often results in mental illness of one form or another. For many people, it is depression.

For mine iniquities are gone over mine head: as an heavy burden they are too heavy for me. Psalm 38:4

You and I were never meant to carry the heavy burden of our sins. Believe me, they are too heavy for a human being to carry. When you can't forgive yourself, you are weighted down with a burden that will literally break you.

Some people develop a case of megalomania as a result of unforgiveness. The American Heritage dictionary defines megalomania as: A form of insane delusion, the subjects of which imagine themselves to be very great, exalted, or powerful personages; the delusion of grandeur.

Rather than becoming depressed from unforgiveness, these people become very exalted in their own eyes. The process goes like this:

1. I know that what I did was wrong.
2. I have too much pride to admit that I was wrong.
3. I will shift the blame for my wrong to someone else.
4. It's no longer my fault; it's his/her/their fault.
5. Every wrong that I do is someone else's fault,
6. Therefore; I never do anything wrong.
7. I am better than everyone else, since they all do wrong and I don't.

What starts out as pride in the megalomaniac transforms into unforgiveness. He doesn't forgive others, because he is too important to forgive them, and they don't deserve it. He doesn't forgive himself, because he believes that nothing is his fault, therefore he doesn't need to forgive himself.

In the scripture, Pharaoh, king of Egypt, is an excellent example of a megalomaniac. There was no one more important than Pharaoh, according to Pharaoh.

Moses asked Pharaoh ten times to release the people of Israel from slavery. Ten times he refused. A few times he half-heartedly agreed to release them, only to retract his offer later. Because he would not release God's people, God sent ten plagues on the nation of Egypt, but in Pharaoh's twisted mind, he was still right for refusing to release the slaves, and God and everyone else was wrong.

And Pharaoh's servants said unto him, How long shall this man (Moses) *be a snare unto us? let the men go, that they may serve the LORD their God: knowest thou not yet that Egypt is destroyed?* Exodus 10:7

This was after the eighth plague – hail which destroyed every tree and every crop, and killed every person and animal that hadn't taken shelter. There was nothing left of Egypt. Pharaoh's servants told him, "Don't you realize that Egypt is destroyed? Let the people go, you fool!"

But we all know the story. Pharaoh didn't let the people go. Even after his own son died in the tenth and final plague, after saying that they could go, he changed his mind and pursued after them.

To say that Pharaoh's pride was out of control is an understatement. When you see everything around you utterly destroyed as a direct result of your actions, but you refuse to change, you are a person who is overcome by the spirit of pride.

I have run across a few people like this in my lifetime. I literally tremble when I see the consequences of pride in their lives. The thought of one person in particular haunts me. This woman never admitted to wrongdoing, on any occasion. She never asked for forgiveness, of anyone that I knew of. In her mind, she never did anything wrong, so she had no need to forgive herself of anything.

This woman was a believer. She had been warned, many times, by leaders in the church and various brothers and sisters in Christ. She did not heed the warnings. She was stricken with dementia in her later years. When she died, her mind was almost completely gone.

The consequences of unforgiveness are severe. Tell me, is it really worth it to hold onto unforgiveness? As I stated earlier, failing to forgive yourself is not a holy act; it is an ungodly sin. Is it worth it to you to become clinically depressed, to the point of suicide? Is it worth it to you to become so elevated with pride that you will stand by and watch your world be destroyed, and do nothing about it?

Listen to me. It's not worth it!

I have heard truly amazing stories of forgiveness in my lifetime. The couple who forgave the drunk driver who killed their child, the man who forgave the judge that sentenced him to twenty years in prison for a crime he didn't commit, the adult woman who forgave her father for sexually abusing her when she was a child...

Yes, forgiveness is possible. It is not only possible, it is essential. But it is not easy.

If you have been unable to forgive yourself, start out by asking for God's help. Tell Him that you want to forgive yourself. Tell Him that you need His help.

I will lift up mine eyes unto the hills, from whence cometh my help. My help cometh from the LORD, which made heaven and earth. Psalm 121:1 – 2

In the next chapter, we will explore in more depth what God has to say about forgiveness.

Chapter 16: What does God say?

For all have sinned, and come short of the glory of God.
Romans 3:23

Every human being born on this earth is a sinner. There are no exceptions. It has been said that the ground is level at the foot of the cross. In other words, there is no one person who needs salvation more than anyone else. Remind yourself that "all" have sinned. That includes you. And yet:

If we confess our sins, he is faithful and just to forgive us our sins, and to cleanse us from all unrighteousness.
1 John 1:9

If I am sorry for my sins, and have confessed them to God, He has forgiven me. Therefore, I must forgive myself.

What God hath cleansed, that call not thou common.
Acts 10:15b

When God forgives us of our sins, we are cleansed. We are made holy by His forgiveness - not because we are somehow special in ourselves, but because He has made us holy. If God has made you holy, you must not call yourself common (dirty, unclean).

This is a faithful saying, and worthy of all acceptation, that Christ Jesus came into the world to save sinners; of whom I am chief. Howbeit for this cause I obtained mercy, that in me first Jesus Christ might shew forth all longsuffering, for a pattern to them which should hereafter believe on him to life everlasting. 1 Timothy 1:15 – 16

The Apostle Paul was forgiven by God, and in his own words, God wanted Paul to be a pattern for the believers who came after him. When we read Paul's amazing story of redemption, we begin to realize the depth of God's unfathomable forgiveness. If God can forgive a murderer, and someone who hates the kingdom of God and does everything he can to fight against it (which describes Saul before he became Paul), he can forgive you. And if He's forgiven you, forgive yourself.

Woman, where are those thine accusers? hath no man condemned thee? She said, No man, Lord. And Jesus said unto her, Neither do I condemn thee: go, and sin no more. John 8:10 – 11

Let's focus on the words Jesus said to the woman who was caught committing adultery: *Neither do I condemn thee.*

It's time to stop living in self-condemnation. He doesn't condemn you. Stop condemning yourself.

If the Son therefore shall make you free, ye shall be free indeed. John 8:36

Imagine how this woman felt when Jesus told her: *Neither do I condemn thee.* Can you imagine the freedom that comes with those words? The Son Himself told her that she was free to go. I believe she spent the rest of her life telling others about the freedom she found in Jesus Christ.

It is of the LORD's mercies that we are not consumed, because his compassions fail not. They are new every morning: great is thy faithfulness. Lamentations 3:22 – 23

How many times have you gone to bed at night, overwhelmed with sadness because of your sin, or your circumstances? God's compassion never fails! With every new day comes a new chance to start again with Him.

For his anger endureth but a moment; in his favour is life: weeping may endure for a night, but joy cometh in the morning. Psalm 30:5

There is something wonderful about a new day, a new sunrise, another chance to begin again.

This beautiful poem, author unknown, is one of my favorites. It was supposedly written by a school teacher.

He came to my desk with a quivering lip, the lesson was done.
"Have you a new sheet for me, dear teacher?
I've spoiled this one."
I took his sheet, all soiled and blotted
and gave him a new one, all unspotted.
And into his tired heart I cried,
"Do better now, my child."

I came to the throne with a trembling heart;
the day was done.
"Have you a new day for me, dear Master?
I've spoiled this one."
He took my day, all soiled and blotted

79

and gave me a new one, all unspotted.
And into my tired heart He cried,
"Do better now, My child."

Every day with God is a new day. If you have failed today, take heart. Tomorrow is coming, His faithfulness is great; joy will come in the morning. His word says so.

If my people, which are called by my name, shall humble themselves, and pray, and seek my face, and turn from their wicked ways; then will I hear from heaven, and will forgive their sin, and will heal their land. 2 Chronicles 7:14

The key to receiving forgiveness is to humble yourself. After all, if you don't believe you've done anything wrong, there is no need to ask for forgiveness. Forgiveness brings healing. When you forgive yourself, you will receive healing. Healing is not just the elimination of pain or malfunction from your body – healing is the mending of your broken heart.

Look upon mine affliction and my pain; and forgive all my sins. Psalm 25:18

Who forgiveth all thine iniquities; who healeth all thy diseases… Psalm 103:3

Pain and sin go together. So many of us are carrying a heavy load of sin, which in turn causes us tremendous pain. When God forgives you, the sin goes away. When you forgive yourself, the pain goes away.

Blessed is he whose transgression is forgiven, whose sin is covered. Psalm 32:1

Thou hast forgiven the iniquity of thy people, thou hast covered all their sin. Psalm 85:2...

Blessed are they whose iniquities are forgiven, and whose sins are covered. Romans 4:7

As Christians we often say, "I cover my children in the blood of Jesus," or, "Cover yourself in the blood," or, "I'm covered in the blood; nothing can harm me." We need the covering of Jesus Christ. The Bible equates the forgiveness of sin with being covered. If you forgive yourself, you will be blessed, and you will be covered.

Deliver me from bloodguiltiness, O God, thou God of my salvation: and my tongue shall sing aloud of thy righteousness. Psalm 51:14

Whatever sins you need forgiveness for, don't add unforgiveness of yourself to the list! God is the God of your salvation; He is the One who can deliver you. He can and will deliver you and forgive you of all sin. So, forgive yourself. When you do, He will put a new song in your heart.

For thou, Lord, art good, and ready to forgive; and plenteous in mercy unto all them that call upon thee. Psalm 86:5

For whosoever shall call upon the name of the Lord shall be saved. Romans 10:13

Whosoever means you! God expects you and me to call upon Him. He knows we cannot save ourselves. If you are drowning in a sea of unforgiveness, call out to Him! He will rescue you, and He will save you.

As far as the east is from the west, so far hath he removed our transgressions from us. Psalm 103:12

Exactly how far is the east from the west? No one can calculate that distance; it is immeasurable. When God has removed your transgressions from you, they are so far away from you that you can no longer locate them. When you forgive yourself, you can no longer locate your sins! That is really good news.

But there is forgiveness with thee, that thou mayest be feared. Psalm 130:4

If you and I have the fear of God, it simply means that we regard Him with an awesome reverence. Once we understand that God has forgiven us, we are filled with gratitude for this free gift that we don't deserve, making it easy to forgive ourselves.

Let the wicked forsake his way, and the unrighteous man his thoughts: and let him return unto the LORD, and he will have mercy upon him; and to our God, for he will abundantly pardon. Isaiah 55:7

Repentance means to turn around. Stop going the direction you are going, and go the opposite direction. Forsake (abandon) your unrighteous thoughts. What are these thoughts? "I'm not good enough. God can't forgive me. I'll never forgive myself." Forsake them, and return to the Lord. God is so merciful! Not only does He pardon you, He abundantly pardons you.

Go and proclaim these words toward the north, and say, Return, thou backsliding Israel, saith the LORD; and I will not cause mine anger to fall upon you: for I am merciful, saith the LORD, and I will not keep anger for ever. Jeremiah 3:12

When a loving father here on earth has to discipline his rebellious child, he does it with a broken heart, but he still does it. It is necessary. God hates sin, but He does not hold a grudge against His children. He disciplines us because He loves us, and then He shows us His great mercy. How about showing yourself some mercy?

And they shall teach no more every man his neighbour, and every man his brother, saying, Know the LORD: for they shall all know me, from the least of them unto the greatest of them, saith the LORD: for I will forgive their iniquity, and I will remember their sin no more. Jeremiah 31:34

If God can no longer remember your sin, it's time for you to stop remembering it, too.

And I will cleanse them from all their iniquity, whereby they have sinned against me; and I will pardon all their iniquities, whereby they have sinned, and whereby they have transgressed against me. Jeremiah 33:8

In those days, and in that time, saith the LORD, the iniquity of Israel shall be sought for, and there shall be none; and the sins of Judah, and they shall not be found: for I will pardon them whom I reserve. Jeremiah 50:20

To a prisoner on death row, about to be executed, a last-minute pardon from the governor means the difference between life and death.   Jeremiah tells us that God cleanses you and me from our iniquity and pardons us. He literally plucks us out of hell. Anyone who is looking for my sin, including me, will not be able to find it.

Then will I sprinkle clean water upon you, and ye shall be clean: from all your filthiness, and from all your idols, will I cleanse you. Ezekiel 36:25

Thus saith the Lord GOD; In the day that I shall have cleansed you from all your iniquities I will also cause you to dwell in the cities, and the wastes shall be builded. Ezekiel 36:33

God is the only One who can rebuild our wastelands. How many years have you wasted in unforgiveness? Let God rebuild you.

For the LORD shall comfort Zion: he will comfort all her waste places; and he will make her wilderness like Eden, and her desert like the garden of the LORD; joy and gladness shall be found therein, thanksgiving, and the voice of melody. Isaiah 51:3

Unforgiveness makes your soul like a desert. Let God plant a beautiful garden there instead, where you forgive yourself and become fruitful and flourishing.

Neither shall they defile themselves any more with their idols, nor with their detestable things, nor with any of their transgressions: but I will save them out of all their dwellingplaces, wherein they have sinned, and will cleanse them: so shall they be my people, and I will be their God. Ezekiel 37:23

To the Lord our God belong mercies and forgivenesses, though we have rebelled against him... Daniel 9:9

Who is a God like unto thee, that pardoneth iniquity, and passeth by the transgression of the remnant of his heritage? he retaineth not his anger for ever, because he delighteth in mercy. He will turn again, he will have compassion upon us; he will subdue our iniquities; and thou wilt cast all their sins into the depths of the sea. Micah 7:18-19

God delights in mercy. He doesn't hand it out grudgingly, a drop at a time. No, He longs to show mercy to you and me. Micah tells us that he subdues our iniquities. Every sin that you and I wrestle with, God subdues without a struggle. That goes for the sin of not forgiving ourselves, as well.

And forgive us our debts, as we forgive our debtors. For if ye forgive men their trespasses, your heavenly Father will also forgive you: But if ye forgive not men their trespasses, neither will your Father forgive your trespasses. Mathew 6: 12, 14 – 15

And his lord was wroth, and delivered him to the tormentors, till he should pay all that was due unto him. So likewise shall my heavenly Father do also unto you, if ye from your hearts forgive not every one his brother their trespasses. Matthew 18:34 – 35

And when ye stand praying, forgive, if ye have ought against any: that your Father also which is in heaven may forgive you your trespasses. But if ye do not forgive, neither will your Father which is in heaven forgive your trespasses. Mark 11:25 – 26

As I stated previously, the consequences for not forgiving are severe.

So then every one of us shall give account of himself to God. Romans 14:12

I try to imagine myself standing before the throne of God. He is asking me why I didn't forgive myself, and I am trying to justify to Him why I didn't.

"Well, God, you see, my sins were just too big for me to forgive myself."

But I forgive you.

"Yes, God, but..."

As the saying goes, I would not have a leg to stand on. As I said before, for the Christian, forgiveness is not optional.

Judge not, and ye shall not be judged: condemn not, and ye shall not be condemned: forgive, and ye shall be forgiven... Luke 6:37

I want to be forgiven! That means I have to forgive.

For a just man falleth seven times, and riseth up again: but the wicked shall fall into mischief. Proverbs 24:16

Take heed to yourselves: If thy brother trespass against thee, rebuke him; and if he repent, forgive him. And if he trespass against thee seven times in a day, and seven times in a day turn again to thee, saying, I repent; thou shalt forgive him. Luke 17:3 – 4

If you sin seven times in one day, or seventy times, or seven hundred times, ask God to forgive you each time, and forgive yourself, each time.

(Jesus) hath God exalted with his right hand to be a Prince and a Saviour, for to give repentance to Israel, and forgiveness of sins. Acts 5:31

To open their eyes, and to turn them from darkness to light, and from the power of Satan unto God, that they may receive forgiveness of sins, and inheritance among them which are sanctified by faith that is in me. Acts 26:18

We are God's sons and daughters. Our Father is the richest Person who ever lived. Jesus is our elder Brother – He is a Prince, and we are kings and priests in the kingdom of God (Revelation 1:6, 5:10). Forgiveness is part of our inheritance! Can you put a price on forgiveness? I can't.

*In whom we have redemption through his blood, the forgiveness of sins, according to the riches of his grace...*Ephesians 1:7

God reaches into His vast store of riches, and gives forgiveness to you and me, according to His grace. He never runs out, and He never charges us a dime. Since we cannot pay for forgiveness, we need to stop making ourselves pay for our sins by refusing to forgive ourselves. We need to just accept the free gift that He offers to us.

There is therefore now no condemnation to them which are in Christ Jesus, who walk not after the flesh, but after the Spirit. Romans 8:1

If we have received Jesus Christ as our Savior, we are in Christ, and God does not condemn us.

For if our heart condemn us, God is greater than our heart, and knoweth all things. Beloved, if our heart condemn us not, then have we confidence toward God. 1 John 3:20 –21

Isn't this the greatest news ever? Even if we condemn ourselves, God is greater than our hearts, and He does not condemn us! So why condemn yourself? Stop the condemnation, and have confidence in God.

And be ye kind one to another, tenderhearted, forgiving one another, even as God for Christ's sake hath forgiven you. Ephesians 4:32

God has forgiven me "for Christ's sake." I need to forgive myself also, for Christ's sake.

*In whom we have redemption through his blood, even the forgiveness of sins…*Colossians 1:14

Redemption is a divine exchange. I want to exchange my worthless unforgiveness for His priceless forgiveness.

*And you, being dead in your sins and the uncircumcision of your flesh, hath he quickened together with him, having forgiven you all trespasses…*Colossians 2:13

If I refuse to forgive myself, I will die spiritually, because unforgiveness is a sin, and the wages of sin is death (Romans 6:23a). God has quickened me (made me alive) through His forgiveness of my sins. I must live in that life and fully appropriate it by forgiving myself, as well.

And the prayer of faith shall save the sick, and the Lord shall raise him up; and if he have committed sins, they shall be forgiven him. James 5:15

Are you sick of living in unforgiveness toward yourself? You may be physically sick, or spiritually sick. Pray the prayer of faith and ask God for the power to forgive yourself.

But if we walk in the light, as he is in the light, we have fellowship one with another, and the blood of Jesus Christ his Son cleanseth us from all sin. 1 John 1:7

I write unto you, little children, because your sins are forgiven you for his name's sake. 1 John 2:12

People who don't forgive themselves are literally fighting an internal war. You cannot have fellowship with yourself (internal peace) if you are holding a grudge against yourself.

And the peace of God, which passeth all understanding, shall keep your hearts and minds through Christ Jesus. Philippians 4:7

Everyone longs for peace. Have you ever heard anyone say, "I really wish there was more chaos and turmoil in my life?" No. Listen to me. You will never have peace in your life if you cannot forgive yourself.

The good news is, you can. Just as forgiving another person is a choice, forgiving yourself is also a choice.

*I call heaven and earth to record this day against you, that I have set before you life and death, blessing and cursing: therefore choose life, that both thou and thy seed may live...*Deuteronomy 30:19

If you choose to forgive yourself, you will create life where there was death, light where there was darkness, peace where there was turmoil, and joy where there was sorrow.

Choose to forgive yourself, today. Choose to agree with God as to what He says about you and your sins.

Then He said to her, "Your sins are forgiven." Luke 7:48 (New King James Version)

Chapter 17: Wrong ways

Are you ready to forgive yourself?

There is a right way and a wrong way to do pretty much everything in life. I believe there is a right way to forgive yourself, and many wrong ways. Let's start by looking at the wrong ways.

1. You cannot forgive yourself by doing good deeds.

This book has several examples of people who have tried to eradicate their bad deeds by doing good deeds. Trust me, that is impossible.

Someone is thinking, "I know I can do it. I know I can finally erase all the wrong I've done by doing right." But friend, you can't. God is perfectly holy, and human beings are inherently sinful.

Imagine a sheet of clean, white paper. Imagine that you take a black pen and make a tiny black dot on the white sheet. Now, it is no longer clean. If you find a way to erase the black dot, the place where the dot was will still be visible; there will be evidence that it was erased. Or, if you get some white-out and cover up the black dot, it may not be immediately visible, but when you hold the paper up to the light, you will instantly see the black dot and the white-out on top of it.

This is an imperfect illustration; we can't compare God to a piece of white paper. But it shows God's character in relationship to our own. God is flawless; we are not. Because God is perfectly holy, He cannot tolerate sin – not the sins that we think are big ones, and not the sins that we think are small ones. Our sins have separated us from Him; that's why we need a Savior. Jesus stands between me and God, so when God looks at me, He sees only Jesus.

If you set out to do good deeds with the intention of canceling out your bad deeds, one of two things will happen. You will either become depressed when you realize that your sins are always greater than the good you have done, or, you will become prideful when you sit down and count all your good deeds at the end of the day. Remember the definition of a megalomaniac in chapter 15?

2. You cannot forgive yourself by pretending you're not a sinner.

In chapter 15, I discussed Pharaoh's refusal to let the Israelites go free. Pharaoh pretended that he was right, when everyone else knew he was wrong. It didn't work. The woman who ended up with dementia tried it, too, and it didn't work for her, either.

There is something very freeing about simply admitting that you are a sinner. Try saying these words out loud: "Yes, I am a sinner." Be sure to follow them up with these words: "God has forgiven my sins, and I stand clean before Him."

It is really amusing to have a conversation with a person who is never wrong. That person is fooling no one. Don't be that person.

3. You cannot forgive yourself by blaming someone else for your sins.

In my book *Spiritual Exhaustion*, I discussed psychology and its detrimental effect on spiritual healing. A psychologist will tell you that your parents, your upbringing, your environment, your circumstances, etc., are the cause of all your problems. This keeps you in a state of perpetual victimhood. All of these things influence your life, of course, but they are not the cause of your sins.

Take ownership of the things that you have done wrong.

4. You cannot forgive yourself by covering up your sins with drugs, alcohol, or addictive behaviors.

We sometimes think that we can fill our lives and our minds with everything else but God. If our lives become very cluttered with addictive substances or behaviors, we won't have time to think about what we've done wrong. Out of sight, out of mind! If I never think about what I've done wrong, I will never have to forgive myself.

Clear the addictive clutter from your life.

Be still, and know that I am God...Psalm 46:10a

Chapter 18: The right way

Are you ready to forgive yourself?

Maybe unforgiveness has been a part of your life for many years. Like any ingrained habit, it will be hard to break, but believe me, it can be done.

Our behavior stems from our thought life. If we can change our thoughts, we can change our behavior.

Finally, brethren, whatsoever things are true, whatsoever things are honest, whatsoever things are just, whatsoever things are pure, whatsoever things are lovely, whatsoever things are of good report; if there be any virtue, and if there be any praise, think on these things. Philippians 4:8

The good Lord designed our minds in such a way that it is impossible for us to think two thoughts at the same time. We may think one thought after another in rapid succession, and we do, but we cannot think two thoughts simultaneously. It is impossible.

Casting down imaginations, and every high thing that exalteth itself against the knowledge of God, and bringing into captivity every thought to the obedience of Christ... 2 Corinthians 10:5

What does it mean to "cast down" imaginations? It means that we are to throw down things that we have placed above God. Anything that we place above God is an idol, and it must be taken down.

And when the men of the city arose early in the morning, behold, the altar of Baal was cast down, and the grove was cut down that was by it, and the second bullock was offered upon the altar that was built. Judges 6:28

Gideon cast down the altar of Baal. This was an altar that was built to a false god. He also cut down the carved statue of Baal that was next to the false god's altar. He got rid of these tokens of false worship.

If you are holding onto unforgiveness, you are placing this unforgiveness above God's forgiveness. This means your unforgiveness is an idol. It needs to be cast down.

Imagine your unforgiveness as a carved statue. Picture in your mind what it looks like. (It is probably very ugly.) Now imagine God's forgiveness below the ugly carved statue. That ugly thing that you are elevating to a high position is above God's beautiful thing that He has freely offered to you. The ugly thing must be pulled down and discarded. Then God's beautiful forgiveness will rise to the top and take its rightful place.

I used to really struggle with bringing my thoughts into captivity. I honestly believed it couldn't be done. Then I received the revelation about not being able to think two different thoughts at the same time.

Try this exercise.

Replace this thought: *I can't forgive myself,*

With this thought: *Jesus does not condemn me, so I will not condemn myself.*

Replace this thought: *I don't deserve forgiveness,*

With this thought: *If I confess my sins, He is faithful and just to forgive me of my sins, and to cleanse me of all unrighteousness. Therefore, I will also forgive myself.*

Replace this thought: *I've sinned too many times to forgive myself,*

With this thought: *Jesus forgives me seventy times seven, so I will forgive myself also.*

Replace this thought: *I'm too dirty,*

With this thought: *What God has cleansed, I will not call common. He has cleansed me, and I accept myself.*

Replace this thought: *I feel so ugly,*

With this thought: *He has made everything beautiful in His time. I am beautiful.*

Replace this thought: *I am unforgiveable,*

With this thought: *I will believe what God says about me. He says that I have been forgiven.*

Replace this thought: *I am an immoral person,*

With this thought: *God has taken away my immorality and exchanged it for His virtue. I am so valuable that Jesus died for me.*

Replace this thought: *I can't do anything right,*

With this thought: *God does everything right, and He is leading me in the paths of righteousness for His name's sake.*

Philippians 4:8 tells us what we are supposed to think about.

What is true?

God loves you and He forgives you.

What is honest?

You are a sinner, but if you have confessed your sins, they are gone.

What is just?

Jesus Christ paid the penalty for your sins. Your debt is paid in full.

What is pure?

You are pure, because the blood of Christ has made you pure.

What is lovely?

You are lovely, because God has beautified you.

What is a good report?

God has cleansed you from all unrighteousness.

What is virtue?

Virtue is receiving the free gift of God's forgiveness, and applying it to yourself.

What is praise?

Praise is your natural response to what God has done for you.

Every time you find yourself thinking condemning thoughts, make a conscious effort to replace each thought with the truth of God's word about you. It takes practice, but it can be done. Life is much more beautiful and peaceful when our minds are filled with beautiful, peaceful thoughts that are true, instead of the devil's false accusations.

Bringing our thoughts into captivity is a part of being obedient to Jesus. You will find that as you replace self-condemning thoughts with God's truth, the negative thoughts will eventually disappear – return to sender!

Afterword

I pray that you have made the decision to forgive yourself. Remember how much God loves you. He has a wonderful plan for your life. No matter what you have done that you shouldn't have done, and no matter what you have failed to do that you should have done, He is well able to forgive you and set you free.

Now forgive yourself, dear one.

Pray along with me: "Dear Jesus, I know that I am a sinner, and that there is nothing I can do to save myself. I thank You that You have forgiven me of all my sins, and washed me clean in Your precious blood. Now that You have forgiven me, I forgive myself. I release myself from every wrong that I have done. I set myself free from the prison of unforgiveness. I am ready to walk in Your glorious light, and to fulfil the purpose You created me to fulfill. I thank You and I praise You for the beautiful gift of forgiveness. Amen."

It is my prayer that this book has blessed you. It has blessed me as well! Please visit our website for more resources:

www.giantpublishingcompany.com

Now ye are clean through the word which I have spoken unto you. John 15:3